Our Tune

Our Tune

Heartwarming letters from
Britain's most popular radio
programme

SIMON BATES
with Martin Dunn

ARROW BOOKS

Arrow Books Limited
20 Vauxhall Bridge Road, London SW1V 2SA

An imprint of Random Century Group

London Melbourne Sydney Auckland Johannesburg
and agencies throughout the world

First published by Arrow Books 1990

© Novelmix Ltd 1990

Phototypeset by Input Typesetting Ltd, London
Printed and bound in Great Britain by
Courier International Ltd, Tiptree, Essex

ISBN 0 09 984050 2

Contents

Foreword

In the summer of 1980, I was looking through the postbag I received each day for my Radio One show. I sifted through the usual requests for records for mothers and fathers, nieces and nephews, dedications for workmates and colleagues, jokes, and snippets from local newspapers, and as I read through the pile of letters, I came across a simple request from a girl called Susan.

It was not a long or elaborate letter, but something about it caught my attention. Susan, who had recently left school to become a secretary near her home in Manchester, had just returned from a two-week holiday in Bournemouth, on the south coast of England. She had been lucky. It had been one of those occasions where the weather had been beautiful for a fortnight — long hot days, warm nights.

During her holiday, she had met a man in a wine bar — Stephen, who came from just outside Twickenham, and was charming, polite, considerate, and just on the right side of goodlooking.

In her letter, Susan explained that she had fallen for Stephen, virtually from the moment he had introduced himself. From then on, her holiday had been filled with the sort of things she had always dreamed of . . . walks on the beach, sunbathing and trips to the New Forest in Stephen's car.

For two weeks life had been absolute bliss for Susan, until that inevitable moment when she had to return home. It had broken her heart when he drove her to the railway station for the long journey home. While Susan's friend carried on her luggage, they hugged on the platform, holding each other for so long she almost missed the train.

For weeks, they had telephoned and written to one another, promising that soon they would get together. But, sadly, it was never to be. Afraid of hurting her, Stephen hadn't told Susan that he had been accepted as a non-commissioned officer in the Army, and was being posted to Germany. And in his final letter, he said that it would be the last time he would write.

Susan was absolutely distraught; but instead of just moping around her parents' house, she decided to tell me her story. She asked me to play the song to which she and Stephen had listened during that holiday: 'Summer the First Time', by Bobby Goldsboro.

And to me it was more than just another request.

I was touched by the simplicity of the request. The story was honest, straightforward, and full of emotion. And once I began reading, I found I just couldn't stop. It was unlike most letters I had been receiving. I enjoy playing requests for people, but Susan asked me to read out exactly what she had felt. I read it out, just before eleven o'clock, and suggested afterwards that if anyone else had any summer-romance stories, they should send them in.

It was the start of a phenomenon.

Within days, I received more than 2000 letters from listeners with stories to tell. They came from all over Britain. They were happy, sad and, in some cases, completely off the wall.

Some of them were almost unbelievable. One woman had gone on holiday with a friend, fallen for a man she met in her hotel in Tenerife, only to walk into a restaurant and find her boyfriend from home sitting at a table with another girl. They had a furious row, a tearful reunion, and ended up getting married.

Another couple met in Marbella, then discovered they came from three streets away in Macclesfield, and had been to the same school. Many were from couples who hadn't been getting on together, and had decided to take a holiday together to try to patch up their differences. In most cases they had ended up happier than they had ever been in their lives.

While the stories themselves were remarkable, it was the response that was so overwhelming. And it was the listeners who decided on the name 'Our Tune' – simply because that's how so many of them described their records. I had more than enough material to run the slot for six weeks; but pretty soon, it became apparent that people really enjoyed it.

The letters became more wide ranging, dealing not only with romances, but also with problems that had cropped up on holiday. I started reading these out as well, and I received more and more letters.

At the end of our six-week run, I told the listeners that 'Our Tune' would be ending – or so I thought!

The switchboard immediately jammed, and within a week the postbag almost doubled. People told me how they stopped work in offices and factories, just to listen to 'Our Tune'. I had to keep it going.

That was ten years ago. 'Our Tune' is now a regular part of the Simon Bates Morning Show on Radio One, as important as the Golden Hour and the hourly news bulletins.

From the early days, after our six-week trial stint, the programme developed on a bit of an ad-hoc basis. We let the listeners decide what they wanted to hear. At first I read out the recording with any piece of sentimental music I could find. Then, one day, I picked the love theme from the soundtrack of Franco Zefferelli's

Romeo and Juliet. It seemed to fit the mood of 'Our Tune' so brilliantly that I have kept it going ever since. Remarkably, I get fifty letters a week asking me what the music is.

Over the years, the letters themselves have begun to change. In the beginning, the letters *were* quite simple. Mostly, they revolved around love, and how it had or hadn't worked. Over time they have become more and more complex. Because 'Our Tune' has been going for so long, people feel more and more inclined to write in and *really* tell me how they feel about their problems. In many ways it has become a sounding board for people – people from all walks of life who just want to share a problem. There is an old adage that claims: 'A problem aired is a problem shared'. I think that is how a lot of people view 'Our Tune'. Listeners can say things in a letter that perhaps they don't think they can say to a loved one, or a relative.

During the past decade, the emphasis of 'Our Tune' has changed dramatically. During the early part of the decade, I was reading out a lot of letters to do with marriage break-ups. With the economy struggling to turn around, many of them centred on financial problems, and quite a few were from people who just simply couldn't cope with life. They told me how they had, perhaps, contemplated suicide – but at the last minute had decided to battle on.

Then, with a widening of people's attitudes on all sorts of issues, the range of 'Our Tune' letters has grown. For example, I started getting letters from the homosexual community – from people who couldn't cope with their gay feelings; and, over the last few years, the AIDS issue has become more and more prevalent.

One of the most touching letters I ever received was from a mother and father – both quite elderly – who had discovered the son they thought was happily married in the north of England, had in fact been living in London with another man.

He had contracted AIDS and hadn't got long to live. Far from turning their backs on him, his parents had struggled and struggled with their feelings, to come to terms with his illness and to try to offer him some support and comfort.

When I read out that letter, the phone lines were jammed. Not only were members of the gay community delighted that I had dealt with a difficult subject, but ordinary people wanted to give their support to a brave, brave couple.

Wife-battering has also become a more common problem. And every time I read out a letter from someone who has suffered at the hands of her husband, I get dozens more like it. Sometimes you cannot help but wonder exactly what goes on in some households – how desperately unhappy some people must be.

Every week, I receive more than 400 letters, and I promise you I do read every one. Although there are so many different subjects to deal with, I have found there is a common thread linking them all. Whatever the problem, people have a courage and bravery that *always* wins through. I have yet to come across a case where someone has said: 'That's it, I cannot go on – it's all over'. But there have been some very close calls.

On two occasions, I've had to deal with people threatening to commit suicide. I have had two calls to the studio – both from men – where they have said they wrote to me to try to get the problem off their chest, but still felt they could not go on. On both occasions, it was simply the knowledge that they had got someone to talk to, someone who would listen to their problems, that stopped them going through with it. One wanted to jump from a bridge near his home, the other to take an overdose of pills. But, thankfully, neither of them did.

Despite all the letters of heartache and pain, there are some 'Our Tune' letters which will just make you feel good. I remember one letter from a woman in the north of England who would do anything to keep her husband. Their marriage wasn't working, she was becoming more and more depressed, and so she began eating to give herself comfort. Eventually, she suspected his eye was wandering – even though, in truth, it wasn't. She realized she was her own worst enemy, and battled heroically, losing three stones. Her husband couldn't keep his hands off her, and they have never been happier.

I remember her tune as vividly as if it were yesterday, 'Fat-Bottomed Girls', by Queen. You couldn't help laughing along with her.

The following is a selection of some of my favourite letters from 'Our Tune'. I've chosen letters from almost every walk of life – some will make you laugh or cry, and some may even sound familiar, but I guarantee that all will fill you with the kind of inspiration that has kept 'Our Tune' going for ten happy years.

I sincerely hope you enjoy reading them as much as I did.

Simon Bates
July 1990

CHAPTER ONE

First Love Stories

Moira and Simon

'*Moira from Hampshire has a love story. It is simple, short . . . and it shows just how dreams can come true.*'
[BROADCAST: NOVEMBER 1987]

> *Let the love come rolling from your*
> *heart*
> *And when you need a light in your*
> *lonely nights*
> *Carry me like a fire in your heart*
> 'CARRY ME'–CHRIS DE BURGH

Simon, my reason for writing to you is very, very to the point. I just want to say that I am the happiest person alive.

It all began in 1980, when I was starting a new school with my brother. We both made new friends – my brother's best friend being a boy called Simon. At school, I really used to like him, to the point where I used to follow my brother around, just so I could speak to Simon. But then, when they left school, Simon joined the Navy.

I knew he'd wanted to do it, but while I was coming to terms with his new career, he suddenly announced that he was getting engaged.

Honestly, it nearly broke my heart. After loving this boy for two years, he went and got engaged to someone else. I couldn't get him out of my mind, and it was six long years before our paths crossed again. He met up with my brother, and came to our house for dinner.

I found out that he wasn't engaged any more, and after a few weeks, we started seeing each other, then began dating regularly. I was the happiest person alive – until suddenly, Simon announced he was being sent to the Falklands, for *six months*. I thought this would spell the end of all my dreams.

I imagined I would never see him again, but for six months, we wrote to each other. When he came back, we dated. Then he got sent to Gibraltar, and then America.

But after having waited for six years for him, I was not going to let a few months get in the way. In April 1987, we got engaged, and planned to marry eighteen months later. I am so happy to be loved by the boy that I had loved from afar for seven years. It is just like a dream come true.

My parents are absolutely thrilled. I had always told my mum how I felt. She had always liked him, and when we told her we were engaged, she was almost as happy as I was.

The Chris de Burgh song 'Carry Me' always makes me think of the time I spent waiting for my dream to become real.

Joanna and Alan

'The simplest love stories are often the best. What happened to Joanna and Alan shows just what I mean.'
[BROADCAST: FEBRUARY 1987]

> *I am the rain he is the sun*
> *And now we've made a rainbow*
> *I think it's beautiful*
> 'TOGETHER WE ARE BEAUTIFUL'–FERN KINNEY

I am asking you to play this tune for me and my husband because we are so much in love, and this will tell you the story.

It was December 1986, and honestly I'd had enough of men, and their lies. So I got myself a part-time job at a local nightclub, working as many nights as possible. I already had a full-time job, working shifts, so this left me very little time to myself.

But I was quite happy about it, because I thought to myself: 'knickers to fellows' – they have really started to get on my nerves. I enjoyed all the hard work, right through Christmas and until the New Year.

I had been working for about five months when, in April 1987, I thought it would be a good time to have a night out with a man. I got talking to a guy in the club who I had seen, and who occasionally helped out behind the bar. His name was Alan. All of a sudden, I found myself thinking how attractive he was.

We swapped phone numbers, and a few days later we made a date. Well, it was just a normal night out. At the end of the evening, he walked me back to my car, shyly pecked me on the cheek, and made a date for the following week.

We went out that next week, the night after that, and the night after that. After seeing each other every night for about a week, my mum and sister said they had noticed a real change in me. They asked how much I liked Alan.

I told them he was nice, but really, deep-down inside, I was falling in love with him. I didn't tell them that at the time. I wasn't looking for anyone special, but I think they could tell by the look in my eyes that I wasn't quite telling the truth.

They had a bet that Alan would ask me to get engaged on my birthday, which was a month later. I told them I thought it was rubbish but, really, I felt in my heart of hearts that something was going to happen. I tried hard not to think about it too much, because I'd been hurt before by men. But two weeks after we met, he told me he loved me, and that he'd never met anybody like me before. Well, by this time, I felt the same, but I wasn't going to say anything; I thought, 'Oh yes, I've heard it all before'.

I took that sort of attitude with him, and he must have suspected, because about ten times a day, every day for a week, he told me how much he loved me. So I gave in to my feelings; I told him how I felt and that I loved him too.

Guess what? On my birthday, he asked me to marry him. I couldn't stop laughing after I accepted. I told him about the bet my mother and sister had had. I don't think he quite believed it.

We got engaged on 27 May 1987, and started to plan our wedding for June the following year. We started house-hunting and, luckily, the first house we saw, we liked. So we bought it, got all the furniture in, and moved in during July 1987.

We were really happy, and couldn't wait for the wedding. In fact, we were so desperate to get married, that we went to the register office and booked September 1987, instead. We had a big white wedding, and all the trimmings – reception, disco, honeymoon. We think we are the happiest, luckiest, most-in-love couple in the world.

We aren't rich, and we wonder how we got everything together, and managed to marry within seven months. But it is surprising what love can do for you when you are not expecting it.

'Together we are Beautiful' was my first record for him when we got engaged. It makes me realize what a wonderful husband I have got. It reminds me of him telling me he wasn't like all the other men. He isn't . . . and I love him very, very much.

Patsy and Jon

'There is nothing better than seeing first love conquer all. And for Patsy and Jon, that's exactly what has happened.'

[BROADCAST: JANUARY 1988]

*All the books I've read and things I
    know
Never taught me to laugh
Never taught me to let go*
        'THE LOOK OF LOVE'–MADONNA

I first met Jon back in November 1984. To begin with, we were just friends. Over the months, my feelings for him began to grow, and when he asked me to go out with him, I was thrilled.

As I was only sixteen, and Jon was nineteen, I worried about the age gap, and how it might affect our relationship. But I agreed to see him and we started going out a couple of nights a week.

As the weeks went by, Jon started standing me up, not telephoning me when he had promised to, and generally giving the impression that he couldn't give a damn about me. I grew to think that I really loved this guy, while I knew that deep down he was messing about with other girls while he was still supposedly going out with me. But because I was so besotted by him, I clung on and on.

Then he dropped the bombshell that he wanted to give our relationship a break. I half-expected it, but for the next two weeks, I did nothing but sit in the house and cry over him. I couldn't believe that the first boyfriend I had ever really loved could have ended it all just like that. My family were thrilled, saying he was nothing but bad news, and that I would get on much better without him.

One afternoon, Jon met me outside work, and asked me to go back out with him. I was in two minds after being hurt so badly by him the first time, but I agreed. The next couple of months went fine, until one day he said he had got a new job. As he was unemployed, I was delighted for him.

Then he told me it would entail working away at a holiday camp in Wales for the rest of the summer, until mid-September. I felt like I had been hit with a brick. I couldn't believe what he was saying.

Well, he went the following morning, promising to write every week and telephone me as often as he could. I sat in all the time, waiting for him to either write or call. And when he did manage to write, all he had to say was hello, how are you, and brag about all the other girls he had met. He came home twice during the next three months, and on both occasions we could hardly speak to each other.

All he could manage to say was what a lovely time he was having, and that he couldn't wait to get back to the camp. I wondered to myself what was I doing sitting around waiting for a lout like this, and decided it was time to go out and find myself some new friends.

During that time, I went to parties, discos, and had a great time. Then, in September, Jon came back home for good. I was determined to say to him that this time it was all over, and that I was not going to have him ruin my life for me again. I'd had enough heartache, but as soon as I saw him, I realized that I really did love him, and there was no way I was going to let go of him this time.

Weeks passed by, and we settled down together, until Christmas of 1985, when he said he was going to spend the holiday at his aunt's house in Newcastle. Thinking no more of it, I went out with a view to having a really good Christmas, thinking we had a good relationship going at long last.

Then, on Christmas Eve, I went for a drink in Jon's local, and found out that practically everybody except me knew that he had gone back to spend Christmas at the holiday camp again. I was shattered. I sat there and drank myself silly, and cried and cried and cried. I felt that my whole world was falling in around me. I wondered how anybody could love anyone so much, give them so much love, and all for him to laugh it off and make a complete fool out of me.

I went on for the rest of Christmas and the New Year, trying to put on a brave face, telling people that he had gone away to his relations for the holiday. When he arrived back, we discussed everything that had gone on, and he said he was sorry for the way he had hurt me so badly over the past year.

He told me that all he wanted to do was settle down and get engaged, and that he realized what a big mistake he had made. It was only me he truly loved. He said he hadn't realized what hurt he had been putting me through.

We have been together now for three years, and we are both more in love with each other than we have ever been. We both understand that we have made mistakes in our past, and that we have to put it all behind us.

He now realizes he was too easily led astray by other people. We are now known as the 'perfect couple'.

Wherever I am, Jon is there. We couldn't ask for a better, loving relationship than we have now.

Jon is my life, and without him I wouldn't be able to go on. He has grown from a really immature teenager into a kind, loving and generous young man. We are getting married in a few months.

Please play Madonna's 'The Look of Love' – this is our record and our story.

Ingrid and John

'It's amazing sometimes how someone outside a relationship can spot what's wrong. Ingrid and John have her mother to thank for making them realize what they really had.'

[BROADCAST: JANUARY 1989]

> *Tonight it's very clear*
> *As we are lying here*
> *There are so many things I want to say*
> 'THE GLORY OF LOVE'–PETER CETERA

My story, Simon, taught me and my fiancé never to take each other for granted, and to fight rumours and false accusations if they ever threaten our love.

It started nearly three years ago, when I was fifteen years old. I lived in a pub with my parents, and, in time, met this lovely guy called John. Two and a half years passed, and then the trouble started.

I had taken up a part-time bar job at another local pub, because we were desperately saving for a place of our own. Well, working behind the bar, you get to meet all sorts of people. The usual crowd, you could have a laugh and a joke with; but, there suddenly appeared on the scene a certain lad called Paul, who used to sit at the bar and chat to me. He clearly showed how interested he was in me, and told me that he would go to any length to split up John and I.

Well, I suppose I was blinded by someone showing an interest in me after being with the same person for almost three years. The arguments started and the rumours began. People started to recognize Paul's interest in me, and started to spread vicious rumours whenever we used to talk.

Well, John fell ill, and I nursed him whenever I could. But I still had to work my usual hours, and every night that I worked, Paul came into the pub. One night he gave me a lift home.

So, when John came back to the pub, people started talking to him and telling him that they had reason to believe that I was two-timing him. Although John said he believed that nothing was going on, he still had niggling doubts, and then the real arguments started.

In an indirect sort of way he accused me of going out with Paul. Of course I denied it, as nothing had happened. But the rows got so bad, I couldn't take it any more, and we got close to splitting up. We were literally at the point of ending almost three years of a perfectly good relationship.

It was then that my mother stepped in. She told us both to stop being so pig-headed, and that it had to work both ways – we both had to give, and we both had to trust each other.

She brought to light the fact that what Paul was doing was trying to poison our relationship, to make us argue more, and make it less likely for us to regain the confidence and trust we had once shared. This was where we began to realize that what mum said was true. After a tearful reconciliation, we began to prove to everyone, as well as to ourselves, that things could be worked out.

We have now got to the stage where we realize that our love for each other can withstand obstacles that are pushed in our way, and if we work at it together, we can stick together, and enjoy many happy years together as we had done before. . . . 'Our Tune' shows just what love can do.

Matt and Susan

'If there ever was a story of young love conquering the odds, it was Matt's and Susan's. Matt's letter reads more like a novel than a letter, but it's no less heart-warming for that. Today, they have a couple of wonderful kids – and are still waiting to hear from the friends who said their love would never last!'

[BROADCAST: DECEMBER 1989]

> *I'm all out of love*
> *I'm so lost without you*
> *I know you were right believing for so*
>   *long*

'ALL OUT OF LOVE'–AIR SUPPLY

Matt's story starts when, as a newly qualified Merchant Navy Officer, just past his twentieth birthday, he went to a local hospital disco. As the evening passed, the lights dimmed and, in a drunken haze, he lurched around the floor, asking the waiting girls for a dance. One girl said yes.

That dance led to another, and then another. A drink

followed, and the rest of the evening was spent together, dancing and chatting, until, all too soon, it was time to go home.

Here the problems started. The next day, Matt had to return to college for a three-week radar course, but he exchanged phone numbers and promised to send Susan a postcard. So far so good. But on the way home, Matt got his first inkling that all was not well. Matt's sister was in the same year as Susan at school . . . and that made Susan fourteen. It raised all sorts of questions, but Matt thought, 'Blow that, I like her, and it's up to me who I see.'

Matt went away, and sent his postcard as promised, asking her to see him again. And he got a reply. He remembers the day quite clearly – 3 May 1979, the day Mrs Thatcher became Prime Minister. At the end of the course, Matt phoned and arranged a date. There was a disco, and they met up again. And the next afternoon they went for a long walk. He met her parents, who were nice to him.

They went to the pictures, and then another walk the following day. It didn't take a genius to realize there was something special about this relationship. Of course, Susan was still at school, but at weekends they would go out. Throughout this time, Susan's parents were extremely clever. They realized the worst thing they could do would be to forbid their daughter from seeing Matt. Instead, they did exactly the opposite – welcoming him into the house, inviting him for lunch, making him feel at home.

But, nothing lasts forever, and that is certainly true of a seaman's leave. The day dawned when Matt had to return to sea. He explained to Susan that it was only for four months, and that he would be true. But to a fifteen-year-old girl, as she was now, four months was a lifetime. However, she promised she would wait for him, and write every day.

As the weeks drew into months, Susan began to feel like a wallflower. Friends were going out on dates, enjoying themselves at discos. She felt vulnerable, and sooner or later a person came along who noticed her – *he* was there and Matt wasn't.

It wasn't an easy letter for her to write. 'Dear John' letters never are. Matt still has that letter, and says, looking back, that the days after he received it were the darkest he had known in his life. His life was empty, and he just felt as though nothing would ever be right again.

Then, one autumn night, on watch in a North Sea storm, there was a break in the clouds, and he saw Sirius, the brightest star in the sky, rising out of the dark. Matt tapped the barometer, and the needle swung from 'Change' to 'Set Fair'.

Almost at once, he felt as though a weight had been lifted from his shoulders. Whatever had been wrong, it no longer was, and he knew that whatever life had in store, he'd just have to get on with it. A few weeks later, Matt finished the tour on his ship and went home. Susan rang, she wanted to talk – could they still be friends?

They met, walked and talked. They covered a lifetime with their words, and realized that they *were* both right for each other. Well, life in the Merchant Navy isn't easy, and separation doesn't get any easier. But Matt said, 'If your relationship can survive the sea, it can survive anything.'

Even though their relationship was strong, Matt couldn't be sure it was love, and deep down he worried. Then, one evening in 1981, they were dancing at a party, when Matt began to cry. He just hung on to

Susan and sobbed. Susan hugged him and asked him what was wrong.

'Nothing,' he replied. 'I've just realized how much I love you, and don't ever want to lose you.'

The song they were dancing to was 'All Out of Love', by Air Supply. One thing led to another – engagement was followed by marriage, and Susan now has two wonderful sons.

Today they look back to when they married, and those who said it wouldn't last. One of Matt's friends even bet a tenner that it wouldn't last six months. It is now seven years since they married.

It hasn't been easy, but Matt and Susan believe marriages can be made in heaven – and this was certainly one.

Dee

'First love is always the most difficult to deal with. Dee found that out. But she also found out how easy it is to beat those first-love blues.'

[BROADCAST: FEBRUARY 1989]

> *So close*
> *Just as close as I can get*
> *The rain and your worry can't affect*
> *what I feel*
> 'DINNER WITH GERSHWIN'–DONNA SUMMER

I am nineteen years old, and the story I want to tell is not unusual or devastating. It is very common among

29

young people. And that is the main reason I am writing it.

When I was fifteen and in my final year at school, I was very shy among boys, and never had a real boyfriend. Most girls in my year had boyfriends, so I felt there was something wrong with me.

If I ever had the chance to be with a boy, I would clam up. There was one boy in particular who I liked, but I could never pluck up enough courage to talk to him. I lacked confidence in myself. I considered myself unattractive. By the time I left school, I still hadn't had a boyfriend, and this used to really depress me.

But, over the following months, I began to go out more. I had my hairstyle changed, which I was told made a world of difference to my appearance. This gave my confidence a big boost. I realized that I wasn't as unattractive as I thought.

In fact, I began to attract quite a lot of attention from boys, but I had not overcome one obstacle as far as the opposite sex was concerned. If a boy approached me, I would appear stand-offish. This was due to my shyness, and I hated myself for it.

I was sixteen and a half before I even kissed a boy. Eventually, I began to make a few new friends, and as a few of those were boys, I began to realize they were not the monsters I thought they were. I was surprised to find out that they were just as friendly and easy to talk to as my girlfriends were.

That winter, I developed a deep crush on a boy I knew well. The big problem was that he had a girlfriend, with whom I was also very friendly. I was convinced I was in love with him, and the thought that I couldn't have him tormented me.

I had to confide it all in another friend, who was very understanding. I had no intention of trying to split up the couple. I'm not that type of person. I hated myself for feeling the way I did, but there was nothing I could do about it. Only my best friend and I knew.

Anyway, you can imagine how I felt when, one day some months later, I heard that they had split up. I can't explain how it felt. I just know I was very, very happy. Each time I talked to this boy, my heart would flutter and I would be on cloud nine. But I knew that he still felt something for his ex-girlfriend, so I kept my feelings for him to myself for a while longer.

It wasn't to be. One night my friend phoned me to say that they had got back together again. I was heartbroken. All my dreams were shattered. I cried myself to sleep that night. I felt lousy for weeks, and wanted to cry my heart out.

From then on, things began to look up. Eventually I got over this lad, and I began to enjoy myself more. Before long, I had my first real boyfriend. I was seventeen by then, and getting pretty desperate.

I realize now that I only went out with this boy for the sake of having a boyfriend. I liked him, but deep down I knew that he wasn't my type. When we finished, it was a big relief. From then on, I enjoyed myself more and more. I had no intention of looking for another boyfriend; I enjoyed being young, free and single.

Then, of course, the inevitable happened. A certain boy took an interest in me. At first I played it cool, as I wasn't sure that I wanted to be involved with anybody. But he persevered – thank goodness! We began going out together. Almost from the start I knew that he was different to any other boy I had been involved with. We began a steady relationship, and we are now very happy together.

I now realize that there was no reason for me to worry the way I did. If only I had known then what I know now. I just want to tell all teenagers who are fretting, to be patient, enjoy life, and some day someone will come along who you will love and who will love you back.

Clive and Christy

'Nothing ever touches the heart quite like an old-fashioned love story. This letter – from Clive – made me realize you can't beat true romance.'
[BROADCAST: APRIL 1990]

> *Babe I love you so, I want you to*
> *know*
> *That I'm gonna miss your love*
> *The minute you walk out that door*
'PLEASE DON'T GO'–KC & THE SUNSHINE BAND

This begins in April 1988, when I walked into my local after working late on a job away from home. I started chatting to my friends, as I had been away all week and wanted to know what was going on. On the opposite bar, chatting to a local flyboy, was a most charming blonde girl, with a girl I had seen in the pub before. Apart from the odd glance, there was nothing said – until, on the way out, her friend told me that the blonde girl liked me.

She laughed, and my half-drunken response was: 'I can cure that, here's my telephone number.'

I thought that was all that I was going to hear from the unknown girl, but to my surprise, she phoned the next afternoon, and that evening we went for a drink, and got on really well.

This is where things become a little difficult. She was

heavily involved with another fellow. I was to go to a remote part of North Africa to work, and although I felt she was someone special, after only a few meetings, our situation didn't let anything start.

I went away, and we agreed to stay friends. It became apparent that the other guy was a problem for her, and Christine – or Christy, as she is often known – needed a friend. By then we were close friends, and I knew that I loved Christy more than anybody ever before.

You probably think that we got together and lived happily ever after, but because we had always said we were just good friends, I never told Christy how I had been feeling over the last few months. I was also changing my job at that time. I had applied to join the Army as an officer. As a friend, Christy supported me, as she loved the forces, and her father was an ex-Marine.

On Valentine's Day we went out to dinner, and I have never seen a woman look so beautiful as she did that night. Ironically, that was the day I got notice that I had passed all the tests, and was on my way to Sandhurst Military Academy, starting in May 1989.

I felt so mixed up. I had a fantastic career ahead, but was without the only woman I had ever loved. We went away for a weekend in Wales, and I then told Christy how I felt. To my amazement, she felt the same, and had not said anything because she thought that I had not been interested.

We bought each other a token of our love, as we needed something to have when I went to join up in three weeks' time. They were the best three weeks of my life. Christy moved into my flat, and we made the best of the time left.

The training at Sandhurst is very intense, and it would have been a very long time until we could have got together again. Christy was very upset on the day I left. We stood in the kitchen, holding each other like something out of a film. It was like one of us should say something that would stop me from going, but all the time we said nothing.

I would have given anything to have stayed, but everyone was congratulating me on going to Sandhurst. I kept the stiff upper lip because we both knew I had to go. She never looked back, and I went. It was a boiling hot day in May.

I felt like a boy waving goodbye to mum and dad on the first day of infants' school. Life was not easy. As you can imagine, Sandhurst is no holiday camp. You need to be totally committed to survive there, and to have Christy on my mind all the time was impossible. Next, the letters started arriving from her, and this made life too much to take. After three weeks, I approached my colour sergeant, and told him my trouble. Getting out of the place is almost as difficult as getting in. They were not too keen on my request. They want to ensure that you are not making a mistake, as they spend a great deal of time with you. They were very good though, and only a couple of NCOs showed any real animosity.

I phoned my dad and told him what I was going to do. He was great, although a bit surprised, as he thought this was the only thing I wanted to do. On Monday morning, I left Sandhurst, and set off to Brixham in Devon, where Christy was on holiday with her sister. At the time, there was a transport strike, but I was convinced I was going to see Christy that evening and that I was going to ask her to marry me.

Despite a local giving me the wrong directions to the station, and sending me four miles out of my way, I finally got there at seven o'clock that night. Her face was a picture when I turned up and asked her to marry me. Everyone in the chalet was speechless. She finally said yes to my proposal, and I returned to Bristol the next day to ask her mum and dad.

You may ask why we didn't say something earlier, but we couldn't, as I knew I would eventually have to leave her. But, maybe if I had said something earlier in our relationship, we would never have really found out how strong our feelings for each other truly were.

We got married in September, and I got another job back in my old company. But with Christy's support, I have now started my own company. We are happy together, and are looking forward to spending the rest of our life together.

The song that means so much to us is 'Please Don't Go' by KC and The Sunshine Band. This was playing the day I left to go to Sandhurst. It started a flood of tears and still does.

I honestly think if you want something, you have to work for it, and be prepared to wait. Secondly, it's always best to say what is on your mind, as you can save yourself an awful lot of pain and trouble.

Kelvin and Karen

'Kelvin discovered that, whatever other people think, love can conquer all.'

[BROADCAST: AUGUST 1988]

> *After all that we've been through*
> *I will make it up to you*
> *I promise to*
>   'HARD TO SAY I'M SORRY'–CHICAGO

My fiancée Karen and I have been together for three and a half years, and we now have a one-year-old baby boy. We first started courting in June 1985, but our romance soon upset her parents, as I was twenty-two and Karen was a mere sixteen. Although, at first, things were just rough, in January 1986, Karen mistakenly thought she was pregnant.

After a really long discussion, we decided her parents ought to be told. The result was total uproar. At that time, I couldn't say in my heart of hearts that I wanted to become a father, and after much crying and sweating it was decided an abortion was the best thing.

No doubt, the fact that I admitted to Karen's parents that I wasn't ready to become a father helped put doubts in their mind about my true intentions. However, after tests, we discovered it was a false alarm.

But, sadly, the next few months saw endless rows and false accusations between Karen, her parents and myself, such was their obsession with a 'no sex' relationship. Things became so bad that I was banned from the family home, putting a tremendous strain on our relationship. On several occasions, Karen and I parted, but each time, we got back together again, proving that a certain 'something' was there.

As a Christmas apart came and went, the problems became worse until, after a huge row in March 1987, Karen moved out of her family's home. By this time, she had got a full-time job and totally abandoned all of her studies.

She came to live with me, but instead of accepting her with open arms, I rented her a room in a 'seedy' house. Sure, she could spend her evenings with me and eat her meals with me, but she had to return home at night to her own bed! Don't ask me why. I can't say — it's totally stupid now.

In April 1987, Karen confirmed she was pregnant. We talked it over and I decided an abortion was the only solution. Even though I had my own flat, car, money, etc, I said we couldn't afford a baby. Reluctantly, Karen agreed and we went through endless discussions with social workers and doctors. Karen happened to sneak a look at her medical report, saying that an abortion was not the answer, but I ignored that. All I wanted was my own way.

In May 1987, I took her to the hospital for her operation. I made the excuse that I had to be at work all that day. But really, I wanted to be away for the 'decision-making process'. Presumably, I would return at six p.m. and it would all be over!

I telephoned the hospital at one p.m. to see if she was OK – you see, I did care – only to be told that Karen could not go through with it, and had gone home. That brings me to the point of the letter. Apart from the shock of my impending fatherhood, I accepted what she had done. I admired her for her tremendous courage. We got engaged and Karen moved in with me.

The relationship between her and her parents is OK now; but, between them and me, it's over. Our baby boy was born at the end of 1987, and he is now one year old. I must say he is the best thing that could ever have happened to me, and the guilt I have, when I think back to what I wanted to do, is awful.

We are in the process of buying our own house at the moment, and we plan on spoiling our son this year on his first proper Christmas. I want Karen to know how much I love her, and all the things in our past that have cemented our relationship. I know how wrong I have been. Without her in my life I would be lost. She is, indeed, a remarkable lady and words cannot express my feelings for her.

Joe and Nicola

'Joe's experience was not happy, but will probably make him a stronger person.'

[BROADCAST: JANUARY 1990]

> *'There's no tenderness like before in*
> *your fingertips*
> *You're trying hard not to show it*
> *But baby I know it*
> 'YOU'VE LOST THAT LOVING FEELING'
> –THE RIGHTEOUS BROTHERS

My story began in 1988, during an exhibition in Birmingham. I should explain that I'm a fashion model, and I was working there as part of a promotion. One of the models I was working with, a girl called Nicola, was on my team. That very first moment I saw her I fell in love.

Now I've been around a bit, and, with my job, have known a lot of ladies. But, this was the real thing, the kind of attraction that great poets write about. Thankfully she felt the same too. During the next seven days, we both knew that we were right for each other. After the show was over, I went back home to Yorkshire, and she went back to London. But it didn't matter. We kept in touch daily and saw each other as often as we could. The perfect relationship.

Towards Christmas, I proposed and she said yes. We

got engaged on Christmas Eve. I have never been so happy in my life. We decided to live together, and in the New Year, we bought a small house in Yorkshire. The marital house as I saw it: a place to live, be happy, and have children. But that's where the problems started.

One thing I must tell you is that a model's life is not one of glamour, as so often portrayed. Nicola, out of the two of us, was the most successful. I was still in my first year, and at times I was finding it hard to make ends meet. It was decided, in fact, that when we got the house, it was to be in her name.

In the summer, work practically dried up for me. I found Nicola having to support me more and more. Things between us became tense. I got moody, she got tired, and she started spending more time working away. This made the times we were together hard. All the things we kept bottled up had a tendency to erupt. Most of this was my fault, but I still loved her, and I thought she loved me. When things were good they were brilliant, but when things were bad they were rough.

As the season picked up, more work started coming in for me and I was getting to be quite successful. For some reason, Nicola started to resent it. Now the major differences between us started to show. To me money is just a means to an end. As long as I survive I'm happy – yet to Nicola, money is the be-all and end-all of life.

After finishing a major fashion tour and coming home, I found Nicola had left me. She wrote a letter saying she needed time by herself to get her mind and act together. She never came back!

One night she called saying she had met someone else and I had to get out of the house. Her new man was rich and could give her everything she needed. I was heartbroken. Did I mean that little to her? Was the last and best year of my life a lie? I went back to stay with relatives in Sheffield. Nicola and her new fellow have moved into the house.

It is now a week before Christmas. She left me nearly three months ago. I've never felt so lonely and so utterly miserable. I wait by the phone, hoping she'll call and tell me everything will be OK. I wait, just hoping she will tell me why, and what went wrong. But there's nothing.

There's no happy ending to my story. Next week I fly to Florida and I don't want to come back. They say it's better to have loved and lost than never to have loved at all. I wish I could believe that. As I said, these are feelings great poets write about. I know I shall never stop loving this girl.

For 'Our Tune', I select 'You've Lost that Loving Feeling' by The Righteous Brothers. Firstly, it reminds me of one night when we both tried to sing it while on the long drive home (our version was terrible). But, secondly, it describes her.

Please read this out, I just want her to know that all the promises, all the love will never go. And maybe she'll realize how much we could have had together, or maybe she'll just call to tell me what went wrong.

CHAPTER TWO
Abuse

Claire and Mike

'People will sometimes endure the most terrible torture – mental and physical – in the belief that they love someone. And they will endure it for many, many years, until finally they can take no more. But Claire's story proves that after the pain and the hurt, can come true happiness.'

[BROADCAST: APRIL 1989]

Suddenly life has new meaning to me
There is beauty up above
And things we never take notice of
'SUDDENLY'–BILLY OCEAN

I wanted to tell you this story, Simon, in the hope that other women in my position will know that no matter how low your life can get, miracles truly do happen.

In 1981, when I was just eighteen years old, I met a boy who I fell instantly in love with. He had been in trouble with the police, more than I knew about, and to put it bluntly, he was a bad man.

But at eighteen, I convinced myself that this man, who was good looking, just needed *me* to calm him down. He didn't have a job, so I took two so that we would have the money to go out.

He treated me terribly, but I still didn't wise up to him. My parents were torn apart by it all – mum almost to the point of a nervous breakdown. I can't explain

42

why I ignored all this, and carried on seeing him, but I did. I just didn't want to let go.

We got a flat together after three years of going out, and we lived together for two and a half years. In that time, he almost killed me. I had suffered a broken jaw, two broken wrists, a broken toe, hundreds of lumps on the head and countless black eyes, cuts and bruises. Why did I stick it out for over two years?

That's a question hundreds of battered women ask themselves every day. I decided to leave after about a year and a half. By this time I had a little boy, Stephen, who was eight months old, so I telephoned my mum to ask if she would take us back.

She was having other problems, and I felt I couldn't burden her. I didn't want to put any more hassle into her life. However, after another drinking session, my man came home and gave me the worst of worst beatings. Then, knowing I would have to leave for good this time, he threw an axe at Stephen, saying that if he couldn't have him, neither could I.

That was it for me. I borrowed a pound from a friend, and within an hour, I was sitting at my mum's house. She welcomed me with open arms, and both my sister and brother helped make room in an already over-crowded house.

I told my mum all the horrors that had happened. She was great. She didn't say 'I told you so', or 'You were warned'. She knew from the look in my eyes that all I felt for this man was hatred and anger.

Looking at myself in the mirror, I was shocked. I was fourteen stone nine pounds, dressed terribly, my hair looked like a collection of rats' tails, and I was a complete wreck. I never realized what a mess I had allowed myself to become.

I started a diet the next day, went to see a lawyer to make sure Stephen's father could never get to see him, and found a job. Within a year, I got promoted to manageress, got down to ten stone, and had a fully furnished flat for myself and Stephen. Life was great.

But just when things were looking good, the company I was working for closed, and I lost my job. After twelve weeks not working, I was a bit down. Then in August 1988, disaster struck.

I woke up at four-thirty in the morning. My flat was on fire!

A piece of coal had fallen from the fireplace, and lay smouldering all night before bursting into flames. I lost everything. But we moved into the bedroom, and started papering and painting, and trying not to think of what would have happened if I hadn't woken up and grabbed my son.

We struggled through Christmas, and I got another job. In my new job, I've met a man who I've been seeing ever since. Although it's only been a few months, we both know how we feel. He's kind, gentle, considerate, caring, and all the things that I'd never had.

We both know that people think we're crazy, and that we haven't really got to know each other yet, so we're taking it day by day. We both know how we feel, and when things get tough, there is a record which says exactly what we mean to say to the people who don't understand: 'Suddenly', by Billy Ocean.

Out of all the things that have happened in life, Mike, my new man, has put that missing piece of the jigsaw in place.

Melissa and Colin

'From the depths of despair, Melissa proved you can find lasting happiness.'

[BROADCAST: JUNE 1988]

> *I've had my share of life's ups and*
> *downs*
> *But fate's been kind*
> *The downs have been few*
> 'YOU'RE THE BEST THING THAT EVER HAPPENED'
> –GLADYS KNIGHT AND THE PIPS

This all began in 1978, when I was still at school, and I met a boy, in the same year and class. We became good friends, and really seemed to hit it off. After a while, we began to go steady.

We got on well all the time, had fun, and saw each other as often as we could. A year later, we left school together. I was living with my parents at the time, and he lived with his. But we decided we would get a flat together – and that's when the problems started.

We both had jobs; then he was made redundant. I was still working, and making new friends at work. In fact, the girls I worked with wanted me to go out with them. So every Friday night, we'd do that – while he went out with his friends. But the rest of the week, we'd spend together.

Then he started to get into trouble with the police –

kept going to court, being fined and getting cautions. Because of that I started to regret ever getting a flat with him. I was still seeing my friends, going out every Friday night. But when I'd get back at about midnight, he'd be there waiting for me. That's when he began hitting me.

Well, I loved him, so I forgave him, thinking to myself, 'Oh, he won't do that again'.

But as time went on, and I'd stopped going out with my friends, he carried on hitting me – for the least little thing. Then the hitting turned into serious beatings. I was getting broken bones, black eyes – all that.

It gradually got to the stage where I was too frightened to say or do anything. For seven years he beat me. Then, I found out I was expecting his baby. I thought that this would change everything. I honestly thought he would stop it. I had the most beautiful baby girl.

But still, the beatings continued. He kicked me, punched me, dragged me around the room by my hair, all sorts of horrifying things. He was still getting into trouble with the police, even getting sent to prison for nine months. Like a fool, I waited for him, faithfully visiting him, writing to him every day, until he came out.

The first few weeks after he came out were wonderful. Then he started his beatings again, even in front of our baby. She was now beginning to realize what was happening to her mum, but *still* I was too frightened to leave, so I kept on taking it from him.

It got to the stage where I even begged him to hit me when the baby was in bed, but he never listened. It was like enjoyment to him. I had no one to help me; I couldn't tell anybody because I was so scared. I lived in fear.

It was only a little time before the obvious happened. I thought, 'I'll never get away from this', so I took a major overdose. I was rushed to hospital, where I had my stomach pumped, and was kept for a couple of days. When I got home, he began his beatings again.

I was under six stone in weight, through nerves. I overdosed again, this time aiming to succeed. I didn't, but this time, a social worker was brought in. I ended up telling her everything. They got me out of town, with my baby, into a battered women's hostel. I lived there for seven months.

In the fourth month, I met another man, Colin. Well, I couldn't commit myself straight away, because I felt I couldn't trust another man.

He was six years younger than me, but eventually we grew closer and closer, and finally fell in love. I got out of the hostel, and was given a new house in a new town where I could start a new life. And that's just what I have done, thanks to Colin.

He's wonderful. He treats my daughter as if she were his own. Now, we're still going strong, and are so happy together, especially my little girl. Although my previous man knows where I am, and who I'm with, he's now living with another lady.

But I've chosen 'You're the Best Thing that's Ever Happened', by Gladys Knight, because it was Colin who made me realize that men aren't all the same, and that life really *can* be worth living.

And Simon, if there are any women out there going through what I went through, please tell them to get help. Even though you think there's no one there to help you, believe me there is.

Trish

'Time – and love – are great healers. Trish's story shows you how.'

[BROADCAST: FEBRUARY 1988]

> My parties have all the big names
> And I greet them with the widest smile
> Tell them how my life is one big
> adventure

'BIG TIME'–PETER GABRIEL

I went out to a disco with a few friends, and met a man called David. I was only seventeen, and he asked me out for a drink the next night. Well, I went, and after that we started seeing a lot of each other.

After a couple of months, we fell in love, and he asked me to marry him. My answer was yes. As it was my eighteenth birthday that August, and we were having a big party, we decided to announce the engagement then.

Well, you would have thought that would be a happy ending. But David had a problem. A problem that no one could help him with but himself. He was an alcoholic.

I tried so hard to help him when I found out, but he wouldn't face it. I took him to Alcoholics Anonymous meetings, but he just didn't want to know. When I discovered he had a bottle of Scotch in my bedroom, I

48

threw it away. That led to his being violent towards me.

He was such a different person in front of my family, but once we were by ourselves, he would be like a monster. I couldn't tell anyone, and I didn't dare tell my parents, because no matter how hard he hit me, I still loved him.

A year went by, and he got worse. When I told him I didn't want to go on, he promised he'd stop. Then, a couple of days later, he'd be drunk again. My bedroom was full of hidden, empty bottles, and one day I told him that if he didn't stop, I'd take them all to my parents and show them.

When I said that, he went mad, and smashed an empty can of lager in my face, splitting my nose. I went to hospital, but as usual, I covered up for him like I'd done all the other times when I was black and blue. I took so much that, even now, no one knows how hard it was and how much I went through.

We had booked a holiday and were due to leave the day after my nineteenth birthday. I wasn't looking forward to it, but it was too late to say I didn't want to go, without questions being asked.

On the day of my birthday, I was packing my case. David had promised to be good, but suddenly he disappeared. My mum had come round to bring me a card and present. We were talking and she was helping me, when the door burst open. There stood David. He was drunk, and we started arguing about it.

This time, however, it was in front of my mum. He started hitting me, and when my mum tried to help me, he turned on her. Well, that was that. After he realized what he had done, he ran upstairs, got his stuff, and ran out.

My mum thought I was just a bit upset at first, and started cancelling the holiday. But I was worse than that, Simon, I was having a nervous breakdown. What a birthday present! I was rushed to the doctor, and he told my mum that I had taken so much, and kept so much secret, that it had made me mentally suffer.

I was rushed away to my grandparents at the seaside for a week or so, but I don't remember any of it. I was so drugged up, and what I've been told is that I was violent, moody, suicidal and very depressed. But I pulled through with a lot of help.

Well, that was a couple of years ago now. I'm now twenty-one, and have been going out with a guy called Peter. At first, it was hard to show any feelings to him, and my parents were a bit worried. But Peter was patient, and we've been going with each other for two years. Without my family, I would still probably be in my terrible situation. And without Peter, I wouldn't have realized what I had missed. I love him now with all my heart.

Philippa

'Philippa has found the greatest gift of all – forgiveness for someone who did the most terrible things to her.'
[BROADCAST: NOVEMBER 1988]

> *Through the storm we reach the shore*
> *You gave it all but I want more*
> *And I'm waiting for you*
> 'WITH OR WITHOUT YOU'–U2

I never felt the time was right to tell anyone my story, until I found true happiness. Now it seems absolutely perfect. Going back to when I was four or five, I would get sexually abused by an uncle who used to come to babysit on a Saturday evening. This went on for three or four years and, although even at that age I knew what was happening was wrong, I could never tell anyone.

The fear of someone finding out about my uncle's perversions terrified me, because I really felt I was to blame. I felt very guilty about it all. Needless to say, all these childhood days were very traumatic. I grew up a shy girl, and found it very difficult to communicate with people, especially men.

I also find myself blaming my parents because, in my eyes as a child, they were going out and leaving me in the hands of a molester. I felt they weren't protecting me as they should have done.

Throughout secondary school, I found myself becoming able to deal with people, although I had little trust in them. In the fifth year at school, I met a boy who I began going out with. He was my first serious boyfriend and, at the age of eighteen, I married him. We had a great relationship before we married, and I couldn't have loved him any more than I did. But soon after we married, things went drastically wrong.

He began moaning about everything, and began hitting me. The first time, he butted me twice and broke my nose. I was so shocked at him doing it, I didn't seem able to move. But he said he was sorry, we both cried a lot, and he vowed never to do it again.

But, of course, it did happen again. Again and again and again. It wasn't just physical abuse, but mental abuse as well. He would make me think I was mad, and would say that I was nothing more than trash.

All this made me feel very worthless and ugly. The hitting was over the silliest sort of things – the water wasn't hot enough for a bath, or his tea wasn't ready on time. But all through this, I felt I loved him so much, and, being his wife, I felt I should remain loyal to him. No one knew I was being battered.

I felt I couldn't tell my parents, because I felt so ashamed for letting myself be treated in this way. From my childhood experiences, I felt I had to keep bad things to myself, and that, after a while, it would all stop.

But it didn't stop. It just got worse and worse. If I had a black eye, I would cover it up with make-up. But he was usually very careful not to mark my face. I didn't go to my parents very often, because I knew that they knew I was unhappy. But I never let on what was really happening.

After two years of marriage, I felt I would either have to leave or suffer a nervous breakdown. What made it worse was that I didn't have anyone to talk to. I pleaded with him to get professional help, but he insisted that there was nothing wrong with him. So I finally left him, and went back to live with my parents, which was one of the hardest things I have ever had to do.

But my parents were great with me. They didn't ask why I had left him. I just said we'd had a massive row. My mum said that on the occasions she had seen me, I'd looked like a scared rabbit – and so unhappy. She said she had a feeling something was wrong, but I told her we just had money problems.

After three weeks, my husband pleaded with me to go back to him. I did because deep down inside, I loved him. I knew that when he was hitting me, it wasn't the real him doing it. All I had to do was wait for him to get back to his normal self.

For four weeks, he was great with me – considerate, kind and helpful. But, deep inside of me, I had no trust. I felt nothing but fear building up. In the middle of 1985, I applied for a divorce.

I saw him at Christmas, and we spent a few great nights together. I wanted to make one last try to salvage our marriage, but I could see that he hadn't really changed. In February, my decree absolute came through, but a week later I found out that I was two months pregnant. I was happy about having the baby, feeling ready for motherhood, but it was a terrible pregnancy.

I suffered a lot from anxiety attacks, because I was still so wound up inside. I dreamed that my child would have a good father, but I was panic-stricken that I would never find one. In September, my son was born. Little Ewan was the greatest thing that had ever happened to me. My ex-husband was thrilled as well by the arrival, and begged us to live with him.

I warned him that the first time he hit me, I would move out, and that would be the end. I couldn't risk my son getting hurt. I didn't want him being brought up in a violent atmosphere. We had a few rows, but he managed to control himself. Then, when Ewan was four months old, my husband blackened my eye. I went straight back to my parents' house.

I kept in contact with my ex-husband, but told him I would never go back to him again. Mum and dad helped me save for some furniture, and a few months later, I got a lovely little council flat. It never scared me – the thought of being on my own. I felt I could cope with anything. I didn't go out with any men for a long time, as I didn't want to ruin the happiness I had found with my son.

Then, one night, a friend asked me to go out to a nightclub. My sister persuaded me to go, even though I wasn't really bothered. I had a great night out, but while I was waiting for a taxi home, I found myself sitting next to a blond-haired fellow.

He introduced himself as Con. He seemed really nice, and made me laugh. When my sister said the taxi had arrived, Con gave me his phone number. Something in my head told me I should call him. It took all the courage in the world to pick up the phone and do it, but our romance took off in leaps and bounds.

He is a fantastic boyfriend, who makes me laugh a lot, which I love. At one point I had forgotten what it was like to laugh. He is a romantic and very loving, caring and gentle. He and Ewan get on brilliantly. They are always playing together – Con talks to him and feeds him.

I never thought for one moment I would ever meet a guy like this. He is the sort of person you read about in romance books. We have been together for six months, and have been living together for four weeks.

My baby and I just couldn't be happier. These two men are the most precious things in my life. I get so much love and affection, I can hardly take it all in. Only one thought haunts me. Because of the experiences that I had, I am petrified by the thought that my son might suffer sexual abuse. I can't make the thought go away. Whenever anyone is around him, I feel these things right inside me.

But Con and Ewan are the greatest things in my life. I just cannot imagine now what life would be like without them.

Kim

*'People can endure such torment and yet still love some-
one. Little do they know, love may also destroy them.
From Edinburgh, Kim's letter shows how a dream can
become a nightmare.'*

[BROADCAST: NOVEMBER 1986]

*I'm in the middle of nowhere
Near the end of the line
But there's a border to somewhere*

'FOR CRYING OUT LOUD'–MEATLOAF

The reason I am writing this is not for everyone to say
'poor thing' or 'it's all her own stupid fault'. It helps
me assess my own life, remember the pain I went
through, and hope that I can just get on with my life.

I was brought up all around the world, as my dad
was in the Army. I was very trusting of people. I always
thought that if I didn't hurt anybody, they wouldn't
hurt me. Boy, was I in for a shock when I got back to
Great Britain.

It was when I was sixteen that I met a guy called
Garry. We got on brilliantly. Everyone told me that he
was not a particularly nice kind of person, but I was
headstrong – I could only judge him from what I saw.

We spent hours talking and laughing together. I
started to drift away from my friends, as we spent more
and more time together. He had been out of work for

55

five years but, at twenty-four, he was desperate to get a job.

I really started to love him – he became my world. Garry started asking me if I wanted to get married, but I was far too young. So we went on as usual. I'd go for a drink at his house, we'd go for a walk, and watch TV. But all this time, he'd never come to my house. I didn't mind, but I did wonder.

One night, I turned up at his house to find him in tears. He had been arrested on a robbery charge, but let out on bail. He swore to me it was nothing to do with him, and I believed him. Although he got a suspended sentence, I still trusted him, and our lives began to get back to normal. We were really in love. He was my friend, my older brother; he was everything to me. I hated everyone, because they said he was no good. All I could see was the good in Garry.

Reality arrived with an almighty bump. I was walking through Edinburgh shopping with my niece, when I came across Garry. He was drunk out of his mind, with all the dregs of the city. I went to try to get him away from them, to take him home. But he didn't care. He was drunk, and enjoying the booze and the company. I finally got him home and to bed.

I talked to his sister about him and, to my horror, she told me that Garry often did this. Every night, as soon as I left him, he would go down to the city centre and get absolutely smashed with his mates. If they were broke, they would simply steal money to buy drink. She begged me not to say that she had told me anything. She said he would kill her if he found out – he regularly beat up his brothers and sisters. My Garry? I couldn't believe it.

I started to watch him. It was all true. I asked my neighbours about him, and they told me that he had been to prison on numerous occasions. I tried to talk to Garry about it, but he refused to change his ways.

The last straw came when I saw him walking drunk through the city centre with another woman. I ran to him, screamed at him, and the next thing I knew, I was on the floor, being punched, kicked and knocked about.

All of a sudden, two policemen grabbed him – there was the sound of sirens, and people everywhere. I walked away, out of his life, or so I thought. He followed me everywhere. He stole my car, threatened to kill all of my family. I went to Crown court as a witness against him. He followed me to work, to my home, and out with my friends. He even jumped out of a shop doorway on a Saturday afternoon, punched me, and ran off.

He ended up in jail, but then letters came flooding through my door. He still wanted me, but I knew he would never change. All through this, I loved him. He still sends me letters, and hangs around my house. Court orders and police protection have never stopped him. When he goes to jail, I get a little peace and quiet.

All this has happened, and yet I still love him. I'd never show it to him. I think I'd kill him if he ever hurt me as he has in the past. But I love him. I'd love to throw my arms around him, and say all is forgiven. But I know what he is capable of doing to me. All the promises he gave me, all the times I put him to bed drunk.

I'm afraid of what he might do to me. But I just hope that one day I'll find someone to love as much as I first loved Garry.

Barbara and Amit

'For some, one chance at happiness doesn't quite work. Barbara and Amit are happy now – but it took a long time.'

[BROADCAST: JANUARY 1988]

Something happens and I'm head over
  heels
And this is my four leaf clover
I'm on the line one open mind
  'HEAD OVER HEELS'–TEARS FOR FEARS

Looking back now on two failed marriages makes me realize how happy I have finally become. I was married at seventeen, and had my first son. My marriage was an absolute disaster. He used to beat me up, and never spent time with me or my son.

The beatings got worse and worse, and finally, after five years, we got divorced. A year later, I met my second husband. Shortly after we got married, I had a second son. I couldn't believe it. My marriage to him was the same as the first. He was always drinking, betting on horses, and in and out of prison. I was so very unhappy.

Two years after we married, he was sentenced to two years in prison. While he was inside, I went out with a friend of mine. It was that evening that I met Amit. He has given me so much love and affection. I have never known such kindness in one man.

Don't get me wrong, Simon. I hadn't set out deliberately to look for someone. It was just something that happened. We have been together for four and a half years, and it's just like we met yesterday.

Every day is fresh and new. But the greatest thing about it is knowing that I'm not going to get beaten up, just because my husband decides he is going to go out and drink.

I know I'm not going to be smacked around because I haven't got his dinner on the table the moment he walks through the door.

My two sons love Amit so much. It means everything to me to be able to tell him just how much I love him, too. We have bought a new house together in Essex, and every night, I say a prayer for God having blessed me with him.

CHAPTER THREE
Adoption

Sarah

'I'll sometimes receive a letter that not only lifts me up, but one that I know will inspire other people. Sarah – I've changed her name – told a story of real courage. Many lives were touched by her very special quest and, for a moment, it looked as though people would be hurt. But, in the end, it shows how people can support each other.'

[BROADCAST: MAY 1989]

And the strength of the emotion
Is like thunder in the air
Cos the promise that we made each
    other hurts me to the end
'I KNOW YOU'RE OUT THERE SOMEWHERE'
–THE MOODY BLUES

I am twenty-three years old. When I was a baby, I was adopted by two wonderful people. I have an older sister, who is adopted, and a younger one, who is not. Both my sisters and I have known about our adoptions since we were very young, and I have always admired my parents for this.

I must admit I was not an easy child to bring up. In fact, I was quite a handful, and now, looking back, I realize that everything I know and have achieved, I owe to my adoptive parents.

As I grew older, I became more curious about my

past, and eager to find my natural mother. I felt no animosity towards her, and, in fact, I admired her courage, as I always felt that giving up a child was probably one of the hardest decisions of her life.

I finally approached mum and dad on the subject when I was nineteen years old. At first, they felt quite hurt and rejected. But, they too have a lot of courage, and hid their own true feelings and fears to encourage me to go ahead.

I began by obtaining my original birth certificate, and then spent the first day turning St Katherine's House upside down, pestering my local registrar of births and deaths, and finally, the public library – going through all the electoral rolls. But I found nothing, and returned to my flat depressed and deflated. I spent the evening drowning my sorrows over a bottle of wine that a friend had brought to cheer me up.

To some people this may appear ungrateful to my adoptive parents, but I kept thinking that, although they loved me and would do anything for me, there would always be a part of me missing – my past.

And, once again, my parents proved to be nothing but supportive and understanding, helping me to carry on. Finally, after trying other help agencies without success, I contacted the Department of Health and Social Security as a last hope. I was twenty-one years old. Four months later, I received a reply. The letter said they may have found my natural mother, and that if I wrote a letter to her, they would pass it on.

The letter took ages to write, and I didn't know where to begin. I realized that I could be about to ruin whatever life my mother had made for herself since she had me adopted, and for that reason, I started to reconsider my thoughts on finding her.

But, I decided that the whole point of my search was to let her know I was alive and well, and had enjoyed a happy life. I did not hate her, or what she had done. I eventually decided that if she ever regretted giving me up, or felt guilty, she may find the letter would put her at peace.

I waited for a reply. Eventually, one month before my twenty-second birthday, in June 1988, I received a phone call from my flatmate. She was crying so much that I could not understand her. She calmed down, and then told me that my natural mother had phoned.

I was so overwhelmed with emotion – I wanted to know exactly what she had said. She had left me a number at which to contact her. Straightaway I phoned my adoptive parents. There were so many tears on both ends of the line. Once again, I asked them if they minded me phoning my real mother and, once again, they ignored their own feelings, and told me to do it.

They wished me luck, and made me promise to phone them as soon as I had spoken to my natural mother. I dialled the number and waited – a lady answered. When I said who I was, she just said, simply: 'Hello darling'. After that, all I remember is asking a million questions and crying a lot.

She had two sons and one daughter – a boy and a girl older than me, and a younger boy. All of them were married with their own children.

I met her a few days later, and it has to be one of the most emotional days of my life. Her children all knew of me, and I was extremely lucky that I was welcomed with open arms by all of them. So now I knew all about my past, and even my adoptive parents have met my natural mother.

I keep in touch with her and her family regularly, as they have all become very special to me. Afterwards, I wrote to my adoptive parents because I just couldn't explain in spoken words my love for them, and all the love and understanding they have given me.

It was such a happy ending to such a long search. How can I thank my adoptive parents for all their support? I can only say that not all mothers are able to welcome back a child into their lives, but even a letter about yourself helps ease the pain and guilt she may have felt since she gave you up.

I was welcomed back with open arms. My sister gave me 'I Know You're out There Somewhere', by the Moody Blues, while I was searching. It seems to tell it all.

Alison

'There are, of course, other sides to adoption stories. Alison, from Berkshire, was a mother who found herself totally unable to cope with a young child. All she wanted to do was to make sure that a very special young girl knew that she still cared.'

[BROADCAST: MAY 1988]

> *If I should stay I would only be in your*
> *   way*
> *So I'll go, but I know I'll think of you*
> *Each step of the way and I will always*
> *   love you*
> '*I WILL ALWAYS LOVE YOU*'–DOLLY PARTON

This is perhaps the only chance I'll ever have to say something to the daughter I had to have adopted. In 1970, at the age of fifteen, I became pregnant. He was my first boyfriend, and we had only made love a couple of times. I couldn't believe it.

I shut my mind to it, and hoped that all would be well in a couple of weeks – then another couple of weeks, and so on. Well, mum guessed at four months. I envy people whose parents stick by them after the initial rows. Mine didn't! All hell broke loose. The boyfriend, unemployed, and undesirable in their eyes, was told to stay away.

I was kept in, shouted at, and made to feel like the worst person on earth. I just choked up, and kept quiet. Too frightened to speak or stick up for myself, and so frightened of what was going to become of me. The rows were almost too much to bear.

I was told near the end that the baby would have to be adopted, and a couple had been found. After all, if I kept the baby, I would have nowhere to live. I remember, when labour began, being so frightened because it hurt so much. But I was too scared to tell my mum and dad. As we entered the hospital, mum told me not to put the father's name on the birth certificate. I didn't realize that it wouldn't have mattered; but I suppose my parents thought he might stop the adoption.

That evening, at ten minutes past eleven, she was born. A beautiful, dark-haired little baby. I called her Charlotte. I cried and cried. Surely, the next day, my parents would try to help – and change their minds. But no. All I got was the fact it was too late; the arrangements had been made.

So, eight days later, through the tears and almost unbearable grief, I handed over this little bundle to some strange lady outside the hospital. I remember opening my suitcase at home, and holding my dressing gown, which still smelled of my little baby. I collapsed into uncontrollable sobs.

I was so alone and so hurt. Everything at home seemed to go back to normal, but my hurt and my grief just stayed deep inside me. At night, when I was alone in my room, it just burst out.

There has never been a day in these last eighteen years when I haven't wondered what my daughter is doing, or what she looks like. I wonder if she thinks I was cold and uncaring, or if she ever thinks of trying to contact me.

The next few years of my life were a mess. I married my girl's father, in spite of my parents, even though I knew it would be a disaster. He drank and, even though we had two lovely boys, it was a horrible situation.

So, one day, I grew up and decided the time had come to fight for myself. I told him to leave – which he did – went out and got a job, and decided to become independent. I knew, if I wanted my life to be happy, I would have to fight for the things I wanted. Then it all started to go right. I met a wonderful man, who I have now married, and he has legally adopted my two boys. We are a wonderfully happy family.

But, to *that* young lady out there – now celebrating her eighteenth birthday – please, please, believe I didn't give you away because I didn't love you. It was because I had no choice. If I could have one wish to change anything in my life, then I would go back to that day outside that hospital, grab her, run and run and run, and never let her go. I love her now, as I have always loved her.

'I'll Always Love You', by Dolly Parton, sums up just what I think about my daughter. I live in hope that one day she will find it in her heart to try to contact me.

Sally and Donna

'Friendship is one of the most treasured gifts you can have in life. Sally and Donna's story really brings this home.'

[BROADCAST: NOVEMBER 1989]

Oh Donna, you make me stand up
You make me sit down Donna
Donna I'd stand on my head for you
'DONNA WAITING BY THE TELEPHONE'–10CC

This story is about my best friend, Donna, and the heartache she suffered – which, luckily, has turned into sheer happiness. I met Donna in 1987, and from then on we have become very close – almost like sisters.

The story starts seventeen years ago, when she was five years old. Her parents split up at this time, and Donna's mum disappeared from her life. Soon afterwards, Donna's dad became remarried to a lady who already had two children of her own. She was the typical wicked stepmother type, who never had any time for love or affection for Donna. A few years later, her mum and dad had a baby girl, and Donna was pushed into non-existence.

Donna came to London to work in 1983. She had become quite a rebellious teenager, and was very insecure. At the age of sixteen, she made the unfortunate mistake of becoming pregnant. She was very young, but decided to have the baby, and then allow it to be adopted. In February 1984, she had a little girl. She weighed only four pounds, two ounces, and was named Victoria.

We met in September 1987. Donna told me all about her life, and we came to trust each other totally. In December 1988, Donna went to America for a month with her employers. She had such a great holiday, and became very close to a young man called James.

Their relationship blossomed into romance, and Donna found it very difficult to leave him to return to England. Of course, she had no choice, but since then she has saved virtually every penny she possibly can, in order to return.

During the two years I have known Donna, I've always tried to encourage her to find the whereabouts of her real mum. It took me that long to boost her confidence enough to get her to do it. In September 1989, she found a potential lead to her mum's whereabouts.

From there on, I made all the phone calls. One of the calls was actually to Donna's unknown grandma. A few white lies were told to get the information I needed – but we found out two great things: that Donna was half-Polish, and then, eventually, a telephone number and an address for her mother.

We were so nervous about what we were going to do next. I spoke to the Citizens' Advice Bureau, who helped me to make the next move. They told me to get Donna to write a letter, rather than make a phone call. We wrote, and posted it on that Friday morning.

That weekend, we were both going crazy. The suspense was unbearable, just waiting to see if there was going to be a reply.

On Monday, Donna received what she had been waiting for – a letter from her mum, Krystyna. It was so full of joy, Donna was overwhelmed by it all. The way her mother had expressed her feelings in the letter made it plain for everybody to see – she had been waiting to write that letter for seventeen years.

Later that morning, Donna rang her mum, and for the first time in seventeen long years, mother and daughter spoke to each other.

All the nagging on my part was paid off just by seeing the happiness on Donna's face. The reunion was next. That all went very well. I can honestly say that when these two gorgeous people look at each other, their eyes tell the whole story of the love and joy they feel for each other.

Donna has now been reunited with the most important person in her life. She had only four short months to get to know her mum again, spending the last month actually living with her, before flying off to America to join her boyfriend.

She has got nothing to lose by going and, in her own words, she's only a day away, and can return whenever. Donna has been through a pretty tough and mixed life, but everyone – especially me – is so happy for the way things have turned out.

The song that just seems to sum it all up for us is: 'Donna Waiting by the Telephone'. But more important than any of that is that friendship and love have helped Donna find happiness.

Alice

'Despite the passing of time, there are some things that people can never forget. Through all the years, Alice has had only one person on her mind.'

[BROADCAST: MARCH 1988]

> Now I've found
> That the world is round
> And of course it rains every day
>
> 'WORLD'–THE BEE GEES

When I was fifteen, back in 1967, I had a little boy who had to be adopted. I loved him dearly, but there was no real choice. My parents put me in a home for unmarried mothers until he was born, and although we all loved him, it was impossible to take him home.

My aunt had adopted a little girl two years earlier, and my family knew that people who adopt are thoroughly investigated. They were positive that my little baby, Danny, would go to a very good home.

I shall never forget the day they took him. The matron of the home came up to me, and just said, 'Go and pack your baby's things. He goes in half an hour.'

Those were probably the most precious moments of my life. I cuddled him for the last time, I laid him gently in a carry cot, and a social worker came and took him away in her car. My last sight of him was in the back of a car, going up a snowy drive.

I was told to clean my part of the room and go. That was that.

I cried for weeks. I used to look in prams, searching for my baby, just to see if he was all right. But, of course, I never found him.

When I was sixteen, I got married. It was not a happy time. My husband used to beat me, and spend a lot of time away from home with other women. We had two children – a boy and a girl.

We lasted together about four years. Then he just walked out on me, with someone else, leaving me, not quite twenty-one, with a boy of three, a girl of four months, and not much else.

Well, I survived one way or another. I made a few mistakes along the way, but I brought up my kids. I also told them about their elder brother, and showed them the few photos I had of him. I never made a secret of Danny, because I always dreamed that one day he would come and find me.

When my son was nine and my daughter six, at last I met a kind, loving man, who took on me and my children, and we have since had two more little boys.

We're very happy. My eldest son is now married, with a daughter of his own. But I have never, and will never, forget Danny. I still love him. When it came close to his eighteenth birthday, I wrote to the adoption society, because I hoped that if he did try to find me, he would go to them.

And I want to be easy for him to find. So far, I've heard nothing. He will be twenty-one in December, and I want him to know that I'm still thinking of him.

When I was packing his things all those years ago, they were playing a song by the Bee Gees – 'World'. The words seemed so right at the time and, even now, make me cry. Simon, I want you to play it for him.

Teresa

'Teresa also found that it is impossible to destroy the bonds between a mother and daughter.'
[BROADCAST: NOVEMBER 1988]

> *Even though it's been so long*
> *My love keeps going strong for you*
> *I remember the things we used to do*
> 'MISS YOU LIKE CRAZY'–NATALIE COLE

I lost both of my parents at a very young age, and was subsequently put into care. In 1963, I was living in what was known as a working-girls' hostel, which, basically, was for girls who hadn't a home. I was sixteen years old at that time, doing what normal teenagers do. Unfortunately, I got pregnant, and the father of my child did not want to take any of the responsibility.

I was really upset, because I found out that he was engaged to be married. By the time I was six months pregnant, I had to move out of the hostel. I went to live with my Gran who was seventy-two years of age. She was very good to me, and if she hadn't taken me in I would have had to go into an unmarried mothers' home.

All through my pregnancy I knitted baby clothes and spent my maternity grant on things I would need for my baby. Even though I was living with my Grandma,

I was under the charge of social services until I was eighteen.

On 29 April – the eve of my seventeenth birthday – my daughter was born. It was quite a difficult birth, as she was nine pounds in weight, and I was so young. I remember the doctor showing her to me. She was beautiful, with blonde hair and blue eyes. The bond with her was enormous, and I was really proud of her.

After six days, the doctor said I could go home, so excitedly I got my daughter fed, dressed her in a pram suit I had knitted for her, and wrapped her in her shawl.

As I lived quite a few miles away from the hospital, I had to wait for an ambulance to take me home. So the staff nurse said she would take my baby to the nursery until it came. Well, that was the last time I was ever to see my baby. When the ambulance came, the staff nurse came for me and I asked her where my daughter was.

She said, 'I am sorry but she is not going home with you.'

I can never express in words what I felt at that moment. I was so upset and confused because no one, not even my Gran, had told me that I was not going to be allowed to keep her. I cried all the way home, and when I got there I just fell into my Gran's arms.

I shut myself in the bedroom and didn't eat or sleep for days. My social worker came to see me, and I literally went mad, saying that they had no right to take my child away from me, as I loved her and would take care of her. Adoption had never been discussed during my pregnancy.

She said that because I was so young, and my Gran was so elderly, keeping her was out of the question.

Gradually, I picked up the pieces and got a job.

I got married in 1965, and moved to Manchester; this was my first marriage. After a month, I got pregnant and was really happy about it. Then, out of the blue, two months before my baby was due, I got a letter asking me to go to see someone in order to sign the adoption papers for my daughter.

I was quite confused about it because, as I said before, I thought that I had already signed them. I was also overjoyed, because I thought that here was my chance to have her back. I was married, had my own home, so no one could turn around and say that I couldn't support her. But when I discussed it with my husband, he was adamant that he was not going to bring up someone else's child – and that was final.

I had to go to sign the papers. The one consolation I got was thinking that if I could never have my daughter, at least someone else will be able to give her all the love and affection I was never allowed to give her. Whoever the people were who adopted her, I want to say thank you for bringing her up, and hope that she has given you much joy and happiness.

In April 1966 I gave birth to my first son, and in 1970 had another son. Unfortunately, that first marriage ended in divorce. I have since remarried and my husband is marvellous. He has brought up my sons as his own, and we also have a son. He knows all about the adoption of my daughter, and has always said that if he had married me first, he would have accepted her when I had that opportunity to have her back.

It was he who encouraged me to write to you. I know that a lot of adopted children do not wish to contact their natural mothers – some, because they think they are not wanted – and I think that some of them might not even know that they are adopted.

I hope in my heart that one day my daughter, who is now twenty-five years old, will get in touch with me. Although she doesn't even know me, I will always love her. I am very happily married and have three wonderful sons, but I have always felt a void in my life – knowing my child is out there somewhere, and constantly hoping that one day I could get in touch with her, or her with me.

Had my parents been alive, and I had their support, I probably would not be writing this letter today. I have taken the appropriate steps and have registered the adoption records with the General Register Office, and should she apply to them for her birth records, which I hope one day she will, she knows she'll never be rejected.

Nicola

'*Sometimes, the search for a real mother doesn't bring the happiness people hope it will. Nicola, from Lancashire, shows how.*'

[BROADCAST: DECEMBER 1986]

> *I would promise you all of my life*
> *But to lose you would cut like a knife*
> *So I don't dare*
> 'A DIFFERENT CORNER'–GEORGE MICHAEL

When I was two years old, I was adopted. As I was brought up, that fact was never hidden, but I was told very bad stories about my real mother. They were not true. She was just sixteen when she had me, and was just too young to cope.

I had a stepbrother, who wasn't adopted, and I always felt that he had more than me – not just material things, but real love as well.

I never really got on well with my parents, and always dreamed that one day, my real mother would come back for me. I always swore that when I was old enough, I would try and find her. At sixteen, I left home, and joined the Forces. Three years later, I got married, craving love and affection from someone.

Within a couple of years, I gave birth to a beautiful baby boy, and had something that was mine, at last; something that loved and needed me. My stepmother didn't come to the Christening, and, at this point, I saw a social worker to try and find my real mum.

I thought it would take months, perhaps years. Some people don't ever find out, but I so desperately wanted to find her. One evening, exactly four months later, I was on my own with my baby, when I got a phone call from the social worker. She asked me if I would like to speak to my real mum – *that night*!

It turned out that she lived in a town in Somerset, where some friends of mine lived. I had been there hundreds of times. It seemed so weird. Of all the places in England where she could have been living, she had been right under my nose.

I rushed the baby to bed, and sat and waited. I was a bag of nerves – all kinds of things running through my mind. At exactly six o'clock, the phone rang. I answered it immediately. I was so pent-up, I could hardly speak. I will never forget the words or the voice that followed: 'Hello, Nicola, this is your mother speaking.'

We talked for over an hour. She told me that she had never wanted to get rid of me, and that she had always thought of me. In fact, on a couple of occasions, she had tried to trace me. Eventually, she arranged to meet me the following Sunday afternoon. She told me that I now had two brothers and four sisters, one of whom was the same age as my baby.

She arrived that Sunday afternoon as she had promised. We had the inevitable tearful reunion. Quite honestly, though, all I can remember is that I felt completely numb.

Since that day last October, she has not been to see me again at my house, but I have been down to her home to see her four times. Sadly, she rarely writes or phones. She always says she loves me, but tells me that she can never be my real mother, only a friend.

I don't pretend that I haven't been badly hurt and let down. I think I probably expected too much from her. Having said that, I still think an awful lot of her. I've had a couple of letters from my newly found brothers and sisters, but they don't really understand the situation. They think of me more as an aunt than a sister.

That also hurts but, hopefully, when they get older, they will want to know more. Strangely, my mother's attitude has now become one where she feels she owes me nothing. She feels she gave me life, and that is the end of it. But, I honestly believe that she is afraid of my feelings for her. In a way, I cannot find it in my heart to blame her.

People may say that I've got a husband and a baby, so I should forget trying to create a bond between my real mum and myself – that I should get on with my life. But, they are people who are lucky enough to have families. I will always feel that, unless I get to understand my mum, and get her to love me, a huge chunk of my life will be missing.

CHAPTER FOUR

Babies

Mary and David

'If you ever feel that miracles never happen, then Mary's story will convince you that they can – and do – come along.'

[BROADCAST: SEPTEMBER 1988]

> Wouldn't you agree
> Baby you and me
> Got a groovy kind of love
> 'GROOVY KIND OF LOVE'–PHIL COLLINS

David and I met ten and a half years ago, and married just over a year later. At first, we lived with his parents in Yorkshire, while we saved up to buy a home of our own.

We finally did it after our first year of marriage. We had discussed when would be a good time for us to try to start a family, and thought we would wait until we had been married for two years.

In the meantime, my twin sister Nicky announced she was expecting her first baby. We were really pleased for her. A couple of months after Richard was born, we began to try for our family.

Things were not easy for us and, after about a year, we realized that there must be something wrong. Appointments were made with specialists, and we began a long road of tests and operations. The problem of our infertility was with me, and we were told that it would be very hard for me to get pregnant.

Operations were performed to remove cysts from my ovaries, and to unblock my tubes to see if it would help. Then I had to have fertility drugs and injections at certain times of the month, but still nothing happened. Three years had passed and we were nowhere nearer to that person who was missing from our lives. Although we were happy with each other, we felt incomplete.

With each period that arrived – which meant yet again that I wasn't pregnant – came terrible depressions, and the beginnings of rows between David and I. I felt that I had let him down, and that I was a failure. But he always stood by me and never threw in my face the fact that I couldn't give him the child he wanted.

The looks on his face when we saw a friend with a baby used to fill me with sorrow. In 1986, when we realized that perhaps our only chance would be to try the test tube method, we went to see our doctor. He suggested going to the John Radcliffe Hospital in Oxford. We wrote to them, and were invited to a social evening. We were amazed at the number of other couples in our position.

We started the treatment, and recovery was set for 10 June, 1987. All the staff at the unit were really nice, and told us not to raise our hopes too high, as they could not guarantee that it would be successful. The recovery went well, and from seven eggs, five were fertilized, and three replaced in my womb. Two weeks to go, and we would know if we were going to be lucky!

Then the inevitable happened, and my period arrived. The implant hadn't taken. The earth-shattering disappointment was something I hadn't prepared myself for.

In February 1988, we decided to try again. All was arranged for 10 April. My period before recovery was to be on 26 March, and when it didn't arrive, we were really concerned. The staff in Oxford asked us to go there, so they could carry out a scan and see if there was a problem.

The scan was arranged for 3 April, but nobody could have prepared me for what they said: 'You don't need us, you're *pregnant*!'

Timothy Andrew was born on Friday, 4 November at 11.05 a.m., weighing eight pounds and two ounces. Our little miracle had happened and he really is beautiful. Throughout the seven years we had waited, my sister had two more children, and David's sister had one more. How hard it must have been for them to know what to say to me.

The biggest thank you has to go to my husband, David, for standing by me, supporting me, and coping with my ups and downs. Miracles do happen.

Pete and Karen

'*Pete and Karen's story is another one of the miracles that happens so often. Every time I read a letter like theirs, I get a tremendous response from listeners – so I know it gives hope to dozens of couples.*'

[BROADCAST: MAY 1989]

When you walk through a storm
Hold your head up high
And don't be afraid of the dark
'YOU'LL NEVER WALK ALONE'
–GERRY AND THE PACEMAKERS

I met Karen at a nightclub in 1984, and after spending as much time together as we could, we got married eight months later. We had a flat, which went with my job in Scotland, and were very happy together.

We had decided, before getting married, that we were going to start a family straightaway, as we both love children. We were absolutely overjoyed the following May to find out that Karen was pregnant.

Unfortunately, the next month, Karen had a miscarriage. We were both devastated – very upset – but the doctor reassured us that a high percentage of first pregnancies end in miscarriage, and that there was no reason why our next attempt should not be successful.

Towards the end of 1985, Karen became pregnant again. We were delighted, but worried about the same thing happening again. Sadly, at ten weeks pregnant, Karen was taken to hospital and had another miscarriage.

We were more upset this time, and began wondering if we would ever have any children. We were determined to try again, but, before moving to Bedfordshire for my job, in early 1986, we had to get over a third miscarriage, at twelve weeks.

In the September of that year, we found Karen was pregnant for the fourth time. We tried not to build up our hopes, expecting them to be dashed again. But before long, we were past the 'danger point' of ten to twelve weeks, and things were looking promising.

As each week passed, we breathed a sigh of relief, and soon began buying things to be ready for the big arrival. At twenty-four weeks, Karen began to get back pains, but we thought it was only a kidney infection. She was taken into hospital, but during the night, the pains got worse, and she went into labour.

Little Fred, as we had been calling him, didn't survive the birth, and I was taken to the hospital to see Karen. The staff all tried to persuade me to see Fred, but Karen didn't want either of us to.

In the end, I decided to go and see him myself. He was beautiful – just like he was sleeping. I persuaded Karen to go and see him. She is now so glad that she did; we'll never forget little Fred.

After a year of upset, and Karen having to be put on anti-depressant tablets, the staff at the John Radcliffe Hospital in Oxfordshire discovered the reasons for the miscarriages – a mis-shapen womb.

A fairly simple operation, with a good success rate, could cure the problem and, at long last, we were told we might be able to have the child we had always dreamed of. About two months before the operation was due, we were told the operation could not go ahead – because Karen was pregnant again.

The doctors told us not to expect the pregnancy to go full-term, and we tried to prepare ourselves for the worst yet again. The weeks passed by, with frequent visits to the hospital for checkups.

Then, after forty-one weeks, Daniel Peter was born. It was like he had always been with us. We hope that this letter gives hope to other couples with similar problems. Despite all the heartache, it's worth it in the end, just to keep trying. Also, if medical staff suggest going to see the baby you may have lost, do it! It gives you the reassurance that he was OK – and a memory that will live with you for ever.

Finally, I have to thank Karen for giving me Daniel. She went through such a lot for us to have the baby that we have always wanted. I love them both so much.

Tony and Sarah

'Sarah's experience was the saddest and yet the happiest – a woman can get through.'

[BROADCAST: DECEMBER 1989]

> *There she stood in the street*
> *Smiling from her head to her feet*
> *I said, hey, what is this?*
> *Now baby, maybe she's in need of a kiss*
>
> 'ALL RIGHT NOW'–FREE

Tony and I were married in 1983, when we were both twenty. We had a bungalow in Essex, by the sea, and adopted a black cat in November of that year. We were very happy.

A couple of years later, we moved to a larger house and decided it would be an ideal time to start a family. In September 1986, our first daughter Rosie was born by emergency Caesarean section. I had had a perfectly normal pregnancy, but it was discovered that Rosie was breech when I went into labour, and there was no other way for her to come out!

Tony, unfortunately, was unable to be present at the birth, but he was able to hold her almost immediately afterwards and to help bath her. I quickly recovered and got on with the job of being both a mother and a wife. Two years later, we decided to complete the family and in December 1988, I became pregnant again.

Things weren't so good this time. I had terrible morning sickness, which lasted all day, and I generally felt unwell. I went to my first ante-natal appointment with my GP in February 1989, when I was eleven weeks pregnant. I still felt awful, but the doctor said it would soon pass.

One Sunday evening, I decided to have a bath to relax me. I got into the bath and things immediately started to go wrong. I started bleeding heavily, and Tony telephoned the doctor. Strangely, I was in no pain and I like to think I was reasonably calm.

I was explaining the situation to the doctor on the phone when I had a miscarriage. The bleeding immediately stopped. The doctor confirmed the miscarriage when he arrived twenty minutes later, and arranged for me to go to hospital that night, which is routine procedure.

I was allowed home the next day, with the instruction to go to my GP if I had not started my period in about four weeks' time. Obviously, Tony and I were both upset about the miscarriage, but I thought it best to wait three or four months before trying again.

During the following three weeks I managed to squeeze back into my jeans, and generally felt a lot better than I had for months. However, the couple of pounds in weight I lost after the miscarriage, was soon put back on and it was still increasing. I didn't start my periods as expected, and I began to feel quite anxious.

In March, I bought a DIY pregnancy test which showed positive. Tony and I tried to reason it out. It was either a new pregnancy by mistake, or something to do with the 'old' one.

Monday was a Bank Holiday, so on Tuesday I went to see my GP and told him my problem. He suggested I go home and stop worrying about it, and to go back to see him in three to four months' time if I was still worried.

He suggested going on a diet. I finally broke down, cried and said I would feel a lot better if a scan was arranged. Seeing how distressed I was, he promised to arrange for one the next day and, in the meantime, talk to the doctor who saw me that Sunday night.

Wednesday went by without any word, so I phoned the surgery on Thursday morning. The receptionist said my doctor was still trying to contact the registrar I saw at the hospital. I was very upset. Time was passing quickly, and if I did need an operation I wanted it as soon as possible. By now I was even feeling movement in my stomach. I hoped I wasn't going mad.

That Thursday afternoon, the receptionist phoned back and said that the doctor wanted to see me the next morning. On Friday, my GP gave me an internal examination, and said he would refer me to a gynaecologist at the local hospital. Nearly six weeks after my miscarriage, it was confirmed I was approximately seventeen weeks pregnant.

Apparently, I was originally expecting twins. I was relieved to know that I wasn't mad, but had mixed feelings about the baby. What if it was deformed? However, I was assured the baby would be all right. All the blood tests came back all-clear, and I finally had my scan at eighteen weeks.

My problem didn't end there, though – I had a bad case of diarrhoea and sickness, and lost four pounds, and then I came into contact with chicken pox and developed shingles. I began to think it would be a miracle if I gave birth to a healthy baby.

But, in September 1989, my miracle arrived! It was the day before Rosie's third birthday. I gave birth, naturally, but painfully, to our second daughter, Charlotte.

My song, 'All right Now', always helps me remember how I went from despair to joy.

Mike and Beth

'Mike and Beth's experiences are not only wonderful, but show how all the odds can be beaten.'

[BROADCAST: OCTOBER 1989]

> Oh Nikita you will never know
>   anything about my home
> I'll never know how good it feels to
>   hold you
> Nikita I need you so

'NIKITA'–ELTON JOHN

The story goes back to 1980, when I met Mike. I should start by telling you that we are both blind, and met at a block of flats for the blind in West London. I think it was love at first sight – excuse the pun – for Mike, but I took some persuading.

We spent a couple of very happy years, just going out together and having a good time. In the summer of 1982, we got engaged. We had two parties, one in London for friends, and another in Portsmouth, with both families.

Our wedding was fixed for 12 June 1983, and, as it turned out, it must have been the hottest day of the year; it was lovely. The wedding took place in my home town, and my Mum and Dad worked extremely hard to make sure that it was a very special day – one that we would never forget.

We spent a very pleasant honeymoon abroad, and then returned to start married life in the house that we were buying in Essex.

We spent a lot of time and money making the house exactly how we wanted it – but always knowing that, despite our blindness, we wanted to have a family. It was in July 1985 that I discovered I was pregnant, and we were both delighted – especially as it had happened much quicker than we expected. When I told my Mum the good news, I could tell that she was not happy. I had never discussed having children with her, and I think that she just assumed that we would not have any. Never mind, everyone else was pleased for us, and we were over the moon.

However, when I was just nine weeks pregnant, we were spending the weekend with Mike's sister and her family in Wales and, whilst out for the evening, I started bleeding very heavily. We naturally thought the worst, that I had had a miscarriage. I was taken straight to the local hospital and a scan revealed that I was still pregnant, and everything appeared to be fine. After a couple of days in bed, I was allowed home and told to take things easy. The thinking was that I might have been expecting twins, and had lost one of them. But they did not really know.

At the end of September, we decided to take my Mum and Dad to the Channel Islands as a 'thank you' for all the work, time and money that they had put into the wedding. The holiday was a great success – until the day we returned home, when my Mum just seemed to become a different person. She said some very nasty things, particularly to Mike, whom she had previously treated like her own son. To this day we still have not found out why she changed so suddenly; but she made us very unhappy for a very long time, implying that we could or would not be able to cope with a baby.

Anyway, we continued to enjoy married life, and all seemed to be going well with the pregnancy; until December, that is. I started leaking down below, and then bleeding heavily again. On 14 December, I was admitted to Barking Hospital, where I was told the diagnosis that my membranes had ruptured and that all they could do for me was to keep monitoring the baby, and give me total bed rest. I was very upset, as I felt very fit and well, and could not face the next three months just lying in bed until my expected date of delivery (11 March 1986). Mike was fantastic, visiting every day – often afternoon and evening.

The bank where he worked were brilliant, and let him have afternoons off work to visit me. I just felt so helpless lying there whilst Mike was trying to manage the house, go to work, visit me, cook for himself and try to cheer me up. I know that I was very miserable during this period – it was awful for both of us. Our little baby's heart sounded so strong; it was incredible that I was only twenty-eight weeks pregnant.

On 25 December, I was allowed home for the afternoon. It was heaven, but then it was back to the hospital for another week. The following weekend I was allowed home for most of the weekend but on the Sunday morning, 3 January I awoke and knew that something was wrong. I hadn't slept well and had not felt the baby move. I just knew that it had died inside me.

We went back to the hospital that evening, and everything happened so fast it was like a nightmare. I was put on a monitor (when they could find one that worked) but they could not find the baby's heartbeat. Then they did an ultrasound scan, which confirmed that the baby was dead. We were both in tears, and were taken to another room where I was put on a drip to start the labour.

Our precious little girl was delivered at 2.15 a.m. on

Monday, 4 January, weighing a tiny two pounds and eight ounces and just fourteen inches long. I know that Mike was hoping for a miracle, just praying that we would hear her cry. But, of course, it did not happen. They took a photograph of her for us, and although we cannot see it, it is still very precious to us.

We were given the chance to hold her, but I just could not do it, although I desperately wish that I had done so now. We then spent a very dismal day by ourselves, just wishing that we could go home. The nurses came in and out, but no one knew what to say to us. What could they say? It was so sad.

We did not realize that we had to name the baby, and go through the business of registering her birth and death. It was all so painful – a time we will never forget. We asked that a post-mortem be done on her, but they could find no cause for death.

She was buried on 15 January; we were told where and at what time. We could have attended, if we had wanted to, but neither of us was strong enough to take any more.

Life for the next few months was quite traumatic. Our friends were fantastic, although no one knew what to say, and I just broke down every time the subject was mentioned. I don't know what I would have done without Mike.

In March 1986, things seemed to be improving. On 11 March (the day that Sarah was due to have been born) I thought I was pregnant. But the test was negative, and I was so upset. However, a few weeks later, I had a positive pregnancy test and life suddenly seemed worth living again. We did not tell anyone our news for a few months. Once again, my Mum was not happy, but we just could not have been happier.

It was a relatively straightforward pregnancy, and on Sunday 14 November 1986, at 11.28 p.m. Karen Jane was safely delivered, weighing a tiny but perfect five pounds and fourteen ounces. Once again, Mike was with me throughout the labour and birth, and when she did not cry straightaway, our hearts missed a beat. But she was just perfect, and still is at three and a half years old.

In July 1988, we decided that we would like to try for another baby and were delighted when, once again, I got pregnant almost straightaway. However, our joy was shortlived, as on 13 October, when I was just thirteen weeks pregnant, I miscarried. We just could not believe that we could have yet more bad luck. After a D&C we were told that there was no reason why we shouldn't try again after a few months.

We were determined to try again, and in January 1989, I was pregnant again, and the baby was due on 30 September. Everything went relatively smoothly, although my first scan showed the placenta lying very low. Because of my previous problems, I was scanned every month. The placenta moved as it should have done, and things were going well.

On 9 September I was again taken into hospital after heavy bleeding. However, after a scan showing everything was fine, I was allowed home on the 11 September. I was so upset thinking that I might be in hospital for Karen's birthday.

However, I was meant to be in hospital sooner than I thought. On Wednesday, 13 September, I was back in hospital, but this time in labour, and at 8.48 p.m. our little miracle Alexandra Louise arrived two and a half weeks early. I was only in hospital for forty-eight hours and we were soon home and a very happy family.

Alexandra Louise will be six months old on Tuesday, and is just gorgeous. She is almost sitting by herself, and chuckles away so contentedly. She is forever laughing at Karen. Karen is very good with her, and has never been jealous.

The fact that we are both blind has not stopped us having two very normal little girls, and we do not want them to be any different from other children. We do not want the fact that Mummy and Daddy cannot see make them feel responsible for us; we just want to be treated like a normal family.

As I said at the beginning of the epic, I have felt very sorry for myself in the past, but hearing some of the other stories makes me feel so, so lucky to have two perfectly healthy and lovely little girls.

There isn't a specific song that we can call 'Our Tune', but one that will always remind me of my three weeks just lying in bed when we lost little Sarah is Elton John's 'Nikita'. It just seemed to be on the radio all the time throughout those three weeks. It's an extra special song and it summed up our feelings perfectly.

Colin and Debbie

'If you ever feel children are a handful – and certainly Debbie occasionally does – just remember what they really mean to you.'

[BROADCAST: MARCH 1990]

> *I never thought true love would be*
> *Making one as lovely as she*
> *But isn't she wonderful made from love*
> 'ISN'T SHE LOVELY?'–STEVIE WONDER

Colin and I have been married for nine and a half years. He was married before, and has three grown-up sons. He is fourteen years older than me.

When he asked me to marry him, he told me he had had a vasectomy, and though it was possible to have it reversed, the chances of us being able to have children were very slim. I loved him enough to marry him all the same, and if children came along, then that would be great. If not, then we always had each other, and that was the most important thing.

Shortly after we were married, Colin had the vasectomy reversed. We were told that our chances of having a baby were only twenty per cent, but we kept on hoping. At the beginning of 1983, I found out I was pregnant.

You cannot imagine how overjoyed we were. Colin, already having had three sons, was desperate for a baby girl, and, sure enough, that Autumn, little Eliza was born – a perfect little girl, who became the light of our lives.

When Eliza was two years old, we decided to try again, and, when after another two years nothing happened, I began to worry. I went to my doctor, and was sent into hospital for a checkup – just to make sure there was nothing going on that could prevent a pregnancy.

I was told that everything appeared normal and not to worry.

Lo and behold, a month later, I had all the symptoms of being pregnant, and could hardly believe it when the results came back to confirm it. I was thrilled and began telling all our friends. But at ten weeks, a few complications started. At the hospital, they listened for the baby's heartbeat, but they couldn't find it.

That wasn't too bad news, as it was early days. But a week later, I was sent for a scan, and things didn't appear to be OK. The baby seemed far too small, and there was still no trace of a heartbeat.

They sent me home for two weeks to give it a chance, in case it turned out to be a viable pregnancy. I was beside myself with worry, and was convinced that the baby had died.

Two days before my second scan was due, I started to miscarry, and had to go into hospital to have the pregnancy terminated. That feeling was something I will never forget. I felt so empty – pregnant one day, not pregnant the next, and nothing to show for it.

We were advised not to try again for another two to three months, so we waited, then started again. In September, I found out I was pregnant again. I was scared to death, but quietly pleased. However, at nine weeks, once again I had to go into hospital. The foetus had not developed, so we were shattered once more. By this time, I was in an emotional mess. Colin said he didn't think we should try again, that he didn't want to put me through it all.

But I desperately needed to try just one more time. We were told by the specialist that there were no specific reasons for the two miscarriages – it was just one of those things. There was nothing to say that I couldn't have a normal, healthy pregnancy.

So we had one last try, and the following March, I was pregnant again. My doctor was great. I was looked after so well. They really kept an eye on things. In November, Janine was born – a healthy, noisy, beautiful redhead.

Sometimes I just cannot believe how lucky we both are. We've had our share of tears and heartache, but nothing can compare with actually losing a child. If I feel tired and cross after a restless night with the kids, I look to see how healthy and happy the girls are. I feel so very, very lucky, Simon. The song I've chosen just says it all.

Grace

'How can people ever express what it's like to lose a
child? Grace put it simply and poignantly.'
[BROADCAST: JANUARY 1989]

You sheltered me from harm
Kept me warm, kept me warm
You gave my life to me
'I WOULD GIVE EVERYTHING I OWN'–BOY GEORGE

I thought it was about time to put pen to paper, as it
is one of the few ways I can really express my feelings.
Back in 1981, when I was fifteen, I was really one of
the girls. I was always chasing around after the boys,
drinking under age, and generally playing around.

I realize now, as I look back, that I must have been
really stupid. But one night, I met this guy called Alan.
He was twenty which seemed quite a lot older than me.
We spent a few hours talking, and we really got on well
together. We decided to see each other on a regular
basis.

We went out together for about six weeks. We were
very attracted to each other, and the inevitable hap-
pened – we made love. As I was only fifteen, I wasn't
taking any precautions. Alan didn't bother either. He
probably thought I was on the Pill, but I wasn't. As you
can probably guess, I became pregnant.

Because I was so young, my mum hit the roof. She

was absolutely furious, and demanded that I have the pregnancy terminated and finish with Alan. I went along to see my GP for a pregnancy test, to make absolutely sure. He told me that I was already three months gone. I explained to him that my mother wanted me to have an abortion, but he said it was my decision, together with the father, and had nothing to do with my mother.

That evening, I saw Alan. We both discussed it at length. We decided that we wanted the baby. My mother was so angry that she sent me to Coventry.

But Alan was very supportive, and stood by me. I don't think many guys would have done that, but he was incredibly strong. In May 1983, I gave birth to a beautiful baby girl. Little Rita weighed in at six pounds and five ounces. I was still only sixteen at the time, but I was determined to be a good mother to my daughter.

When Rita was seven months old, all three of us moved into our own home. My mum came round to the idea of being a grandma, and doted on her grandchild. After eighteen months, we decided to try for another child, so I stopped using any contraception. Eventually I became pregnant again, and in August 1985, we had a son.

Roy weighed in at just under eight pounds. We had the perfect family – a boy, a girl, a comfortable home, and nothing to worry about at all.

We watched the children grow, heard Roy speak his first word – Da da – and saw his first little crawl. Then, in February the following year, I woke up. I sensed something was wrong. I went into Roy's room to find he was not breathing.

I screamed at Alan to get a doctor as quickly as he could. He raced outside to find a phone, and saw a passing police car. He flagged it down, and one of the policemen tried artificial respiration. An ambulance arrived, and they tried to revive my little boy, but nothing worked.

He was pronounced dead on arrival at the local hospital, another victim of Cot Death Syndrome. We were all absolutely devastated. Relatives, friends, doctors and health workers were all brilliant, helping us cope with the shock of it all.

Alan, Rita and I went into a little world of our own. We gave each other comfort. Alan and I used to lie awake for hours, trying to comfort each other. Eventually, we made love to try to console each other, and later that year I became pregnant again. I know what you and everybody are thinking – that we did it to replace Roy. But it wasn't like that.

No one could *ever* replace him. Although he was only five and a half months old, he was *very* special to us. He always will be.

His smiling face will be engraved in our minds forever. No one can ever take that away from us. He was always smiling and laughing and chuckling.

He would have been three this August, and this song is just a little tribute to him, to remind ourselves – and everyone whose lives he touched – just how special he was.

There isn't a day goes by that we don't think of him. We still love him and remember him. We have another son, who is healthy and getting up to all sorts of mischief. He has helped us in a big way to come to terms with what happened.

But we'll never forget Roy.

Ted and Margaret

'For Ted, the only thing that matters is persuading the people that he really cares for, that he has changed.'
[BROADCAST: AUGUST 1985]

> No I can't forget this evening
> Or your face as you were leaving
> But I guess that's just the way the story
>   goes
>
> 'WITHOUT YOU'–NILSSON

I met Margaret in 1983, when I was visiting my cousin, and decided there and then that she was the one for me. She was living with my cousin in a squat, and I was living with my grandparents in London.

Margaret soon became my girlfriend, and after a bit of persuasion from me and my cousin, my grandparents agreed to let her live with us. We got engaged six months later, and set the wedding date for 26 January 1985.

Six months before the wedding, Margaret went to the doctor and was told she was pregnant. We were overjoyed, but as the baby was due in February, we decided to bring the wedding forward to 10 November 1984. All went well, and on 3 February 1986, our six pound, thirteen ounce daughter Sophie was born.

We were over the moon; everything looked well and we moved into a flat in Central London. I was still working, and had a good job, but we didn't want to stay in London so I had two weeks' holiday and went back to my hometown in Nottinghamshire to look for work and a house, whilst Margaret stayed in London.

Well, we moved up to Nottingham and into our new house in late 1985. And Margaret became pregnant again. On 15 January, our little boy Michael was born, weighing six pounds and three ounces. I got a driving job, and everything was going well, until we both started to go out separately.

Margaret didn't mind me going out on my own, but after she came in from her night out I used to ask hundreds of questions because I was jealous. I love her dearly – and more than anything, but stupid things kept going through my mind, like who she had been talking to, and what had she been up to. Really stupid and jealous things, which I wish I had never thought or asked about.

Sophie was now two years old and Michael nine months. I was paying more attention to my son, and shouting and smacking Sophie. I wasn't really hurting her, just little taps if she was making a noise or banging something that all kids do. I didn't stop to think. I love my wife and kids more than life itself and wish to God there was some way of showing or winning back the affection of my wife and daughter.

I hope they don't hate me – I am not a monster but I promise I will change if Margaret will give me another chance. I don't drink much, although maybe I play a little too much football. But please, Simon, tell her, I love her and the kids, and maybe this song, 'Without you', by Nilsson, will say it all.

CHAPTER FIVE
Miracles

Caroline

'If you have doubts about the strength of the human spirit, then letters like Caroline's dispel them all. This is a story of a family – and one very special young man – who refused to be beaten by the odds. An ordinary family, who simply would not accept that a tragedy could wreck their lives.

[BROADCAST: MAY 1989]

> How can I just let you walk away
> Just let you leave without a trace
> When I stand here taking every breath
>   with you
> 'AGAINST ALL ODDS'–PHIL COLLINS

It has taken me some twenty months to feel confident enough even to write to you. In May 1987, things were very good for me. My husband, who had been unemployed, had gone to London to find some work. He was due back at home in the West Midlands on Friday evening.

I didn't like staying alone, so my younger brother Andrew came to stay the night. He was a caring fellow – unusual for someone who is just twenty years old – and he took me and a girlfriend out for a drink.

We got up for work the next morning. I prepared him a lunch to take with him. For the first time in a few days, there was a slight drizzle. He was going to use his motorbike, which he hadn't driven for a long time. I offered to drive him in my car, but, no, he went off on his bike.

I was going out that evening with my friend, Marion. It was nearly half-past two in the afternoon, and we were joking and chatting on the phone, making our plans. A few minutes later, another phone rang on my switchboard, and I asked her to hold for a moment.

What happened next can only be described as the worst moment of my life. My dad was calling from a phone box, in tears, telling me to get straight to the local hospital. 'Andrew has had an accident', was all he could say.

I found the courage to ask him how serious it was, hoping he would just say broken bones. My dad could only reply, 'Very bad'.

The next hours passed in a dream. I somehow drove to the hospital, saw my dad and stepmum, who were both shattered, only to be told that Andrew had suffered brain damage. To what extent, nobody knew. We were left sitting in a quiet room for half an hour. A kind sister came in with tea, followed by a doctor. We were told that Andrew had suffered very bad head injuries – his brain was bleeding.

They couldn't say whether Andrew would pull through, but if he did, there was every chance that he probably would not walk or talk. They said that if there were any close family, they should be brought to the hospital straightaway.

We were told we would see Andrew in the intensive care unit. We walked along behind a nurse – all three of us holding hands – really not knowing what to expect. We were given plastic aprons, and taken to Andrew's bedside. We had the shock of our lives.

There was not *one* mark on his face, just a bad cut on his leg. He was on a life-support machine, with tubes and wires everywhere, but really only looked as though he was asleep.

We learned that Andrew had come off his bike on a traffic island, and gone under a car, which had caused him to stop breathing. They did not know for how long, but it had caused brain damage and, apparently, he had stopped breathing on a couple of occasions after that.

All the family saw Andrew, and were obviously devastated. We all felt so helpless, because all we could do was sit, wait and try to talk to him normally. The hospital was marvellous. They gave us this little room where we could sit, but I can't begin to tell you, Simon, the pain and heartache we were feeling.

For five days, Andrew was on a life-support machine. I had decided to go to work on the Tuesday, because I felt I would go insane if I had to spend another day just waiting. But when I arrived at dawn on the Tuesday to visit Andrew, before going to the office, they had started to let him breathe by himself, with only a little help from the machine. This cheered me up no end.

On Wednesday morning, the machine was pushed to the back of the bed, and although the pipes were still attached, as a precautionary measure, the machine was switched off. A week later he was moved onto a normal ward.

Although he was still in a coma, it was termed 'light', so we started to play his favourite music, like Bob Marley and UB40, and just talked to him. After four weeks of sheer hell, he opened his eyes. He looked blank and just stared. There was obviously still a long way to go.

They moved him to an end bed in the ward, and sat him in a chair. Although the drips were removed, there was still no real response. All we could do was surround him with our love.

After another couple of weeks, Dad and other members of the family were able to put their arms around Andrew's neck and more or less drag him up the ward. He was having physiotherapy every day, and we used to treat him to sweets and cakes if he did well.

We went with him to the physiotherapy department a few times. On one occasion, he was asked who I was. In a faint whisper, he said: 'Caroline'.

I felt like my heart was going to burst. I threw my arms around him, and cried and cried. Then, one day, I was teasing him, trying to get him to talk. Suddenly, he let out a shout. From that day, he never looked back.

We held a family conference, and my stepmum said she would give up work to have Andrew come home. My dad looked after him in the evenings, and he went to physio in the afternoons.

Things have only gone up and up since then. Andrew now has a job, attends hospital only once every three months, has got engaged to Debby, who stood by him through it all, and, in July, he will get married.

We are so proud of him, Simon. How he fought all the way! Now I take him to see other people when we read of other victims of car accidents. Sometimes it does really help. I just pray that this will give hope to other people who find themselves in such a position.

'Against All Odds', by Phil Collins brings tears to my eyes every time I hear it, because where Andrew is concerned, it is all so true.

Catherine

'It often takes adversity to make people see what they have. Catherine discovered that only too clearly.'
[BROADCAST: MARCH 1990]

And if the stars fell down from the sky
baby
I would make it through
But in a world without you where
would I be
'WORLD WITHOUT YOU'–BELINDA CARLISLE

After marrying young, and divorcing after only two years, I married a lovely man, Chris, who had been in the Merchant Navy. We both lived in the south of England. After only a few weeks of having known one another, we started living together.

We had our first baby boy in November 1983, and moved down to Somerset. In December 1985, after two miscarriages, I had another baby boy, and our family seemed complete. Although we were hard up, we were very happy.

In September 1987, I had another baby boy, and this just made things better. My boys loved their dad, not only as a dad, but also as their best friend.

We both worked, Chris all day, and me at night. As time went by, we saw less and less of each other. I became more and more tired and bad-tempered. Everything that Chris did was wrong, even though he was trying to help me around the house.

By Christmas, I was really thinking I would be better off on my own. We seemed always to be working, but still terribly hard up. Then came a day in February which changed everything. It just started off as a normal day. Chris went to work, my oldest boy went to school, and I did all the normal things around the house.

At lunchtime, my husband came home from work. At one point, I joked I would have to do him in and claim the insurance money, as we were getting worse off. Suddenly he complained of a headache, something he never got.

I asked him if he wanted anything for it, but he just put his coat on, and walked away. I forgot all about it as soon as the door closed. My mum came round in the afternoon to collect my boy from school, and I told her that I would love someone to look after the children for a few days so that Chris and I could have some time to ourselves.

Just an hour or so later, my father came in to say that Chris had collapsed at work, and had been rushed to hospital. I just couldn't believe it. I hadn't even bothered when he said he had a headache.

All the way to the hospital, I kept thinking that I hadn't even said goodbye to him. It was like a nightmare. When I got there he was already being transferred from our local hospital to one in Birmingham – so I knew it must be more serious than I thought.

I just couldn't seem to sort myself out. It was breaking my heart. What was I going to do? I wanted to be with Chris, but my three little boys also needed me. They kept asking about their daddy. I just didn't know what to say. The first night on my own was terrible. I couldn't sleep. And I couldn't get my mind straight. It was then that I began to realize just what I had, and what I was going to lose.

I knew then that I just couldn't cope without him.

Chris had suffered a haemorrhage. But after many weeks of worry, and sitting by his bed, he is now on the way to full recovery. It has made me open my eyes to things. I had everything, but almost lost it all. Our family life is slowly returning to normal, and we are all now much closer than we have ever been.

We've been through so much but, thank God, we can all start living our lives all over again. My tune is 'World Without You', by Belinda Carlisle. Whatever would I have done without Chris?

Matt and Linda

'The story of Matt and Linda is perhaps one of the most touching I have ever read. I have deliberately not changed their names as a testament to Matt's courage.'
[BROADCAST: MARCH 1989]

In my heart there's a special place for
    you
If only for the faith you have in me
So for always you'll be my special girl
'HERE'S TO YOU'–BILLY OCEAN

My name is Matt, and in February 1988, I was involved in a very serious judo accident, which nearly cost me my life. At the time I was twenty-four years old, and employed by Nottinghamshire Ambulance Service as a vehicle mechanic.

I had a steady relationship with a girl called Linda, who I had met through my sister, when they were still at school. It started off as a relationship that I was not too sure about – Linda was fifteen, and I was eighteen. Consequently, this was a target for a lot of mickey-taking by my friends.

At one point, I nearly let it all get to me, but managed to rise above it, and our relationship went from strength to strength. We started to talk about getting engaged, and buying a house, which was, of course, to be followed by marriage.

The year 1987 had not been a good one by our standards, and we said we would look forward to a better one in 1988. But this was not to be. As fate might have it, on 29 February, I was due to get engaged to Linda. Instead, after falling badly at Judo, I was lying critically ill in Nottingham's Queen's Medical Centre intensive care unit with a broken neck and a severely damaged spinal cord, which was to leave me paralysed from the neck down.

Due to the care and professionalism of the Nottinghamshire Ambulance Service and Queen's Medical Centre, I made it through, although at one stage I didn't think I would, and worse than this, wasn't sure I wanted to.

At the time, all I could see was me being a cabbage and a burden to my family and friends, and especially Linda. I didn't want this. Before the accident I believed in having the right to die, and told my feelings to Linda.

The doctors wouldn't hear about it, and set about talking me out of it. I'm now so thankful it worked. The doctors told me what wonders could be done with spinal-injury patients. During this time, Linda was at my bedside practically day and night.

On 17 March, when I was off the life-support machine, Linda and I decided to get engaged, but not at the Royal Hotel, where it had originally been planned. Instead, it was in the QMC intensive care unit, where we celebrated with our immediate families and the nurses.

It was a very emotional time for both Linda and me, and also our families and the nurses, who, by now, were seeing quite a lot of us.

On 21 March, I was transferred to a spinal injuries unit in Sheffield, where I was to spend the next five months. This was the place that Linda was going to visit daily after work, for the next twenty weeks, and the place where I was to learn the hard facts about my disability.

I was taken by ambulance that morning, and escorted by Linda. When I arrived, I didn't receive the pleasant welcoming committee that I had expected. Instead, the staff seemed hostile towards Linda and, at the time, made a bad situation even worse.

At a later date, I was to find out that coping with my disability was more of a psychological one than a physical one, and the consultant told Linda that she was better leaving me now, and getting out of the situation while she could. Linda was very upset at this and so was I.

With hindsight, I can now see why they did this; but obviously, at the time, I couldn't. In a lot of cases like mine, the other halves cannot cope. This is quite understandable, and if that's the case, it is better that they get out sooner rather than later.

Fortunately for me, Linda was able to cope, and my accident brought us closer together, and made our relationship even stronger.

I had always been a bit of a realist, and now was certainly the time to start looking at things realistically. Linda and I had been struck a very big blow, probably one of the biggest blows that anybody could be expected to face. I knew that if I was going to cope, it would have to be a team effort.

Prior to my accident, Linda and I had obviously discussed marriage, and had, between ourselves, set a date for August 1989. Our intention had been to buy a house prior to the wedding, and decorate it so that we could move straight in afterwards.

Those future plans now had to be changed considerably. It was as if the whole world had come tumbling in around us, and we were being left to pick up the pieces. I would obviously not be able to return to my old job, and, in fact, may not be able to work again.

Consequently, I am not going to be able to get a mortgage, and as it was going to be necessary for Linda to give up work to look after me, neither would she. It became obvious that if we were to live together on our own, she would have to find somewhere through our local council, and this made it necessary for us to be married.

So we set about planning this straightaway, and the date was set for October. Linda got on with the wedding arrangements while I was in hospital. I sometimes wonder how she managed to do all the organizing, as well as travelling to Sheffield every night, but somehow she managed it.

At the beginning of July, I was allowed to go home for weekends to see how the family, Linda and I would cope before I was discharged. The first weekend I went home was quite an ordeal, as I went into Nottingham to sort out my wedding suit, which took all afternoon. Seven pairs of trousers later, I emerged from the hire shop all geared up for my wedding day.

If you can imagine Linda, me, the best man and the usher in a changing room trying trousers on, you can see why I was so shattered when I finished. If that was not tiring enough, when I got home, Linda had organized a surprise welcome-home party with all my friends.

I carried on going home for about seven weeks, until I was finally discharged in August. It was rather sad to leave after all that time, as we had both got really friendly with the nurses and doctors. Even though we hadn't been so sure at first, they turned out to be a fantastic group of people, who we will both remember for the rest of our lives. They deserve much more credit than they get.

Within three weeks, we were moving into a purpose-built disabled person's bungalow, getting ready for the wedding. We were really busy, furnishing the bungalow, as well as making all the final preparations.

We eventually married in October. I would like to mention two of the nurses who came down from Sheffield – Joanna and Tammy – on the morning of the wedding to get me ready, so we could keep the tradition of not seeing each other on the morning of the wedding.

We are now settling down into married life, and taking my disability in our stride. Friends and family have been such a help. It is now coming up to the anniversary of my accident. The words of 'Here's to You' could have been written for us. They say everything about our ordeal.

PS: This letter has taken me four hours to type, as I cannot use my hands to write, I have to use special adaptations for a keyboard.

The Johnsons

'The courage of grown ups sometimes pales into insignificance when compared to the courage of children. Anita, from Birmingham, brought that home with the story of her son, Lee.'

[BROADCAST: OCTOBER 1987]

> *Don't worry if it's not good enough*
> *For anyone else to hear*
> *Just sing, sing a song*
>
> 'SING'–THE CARPENTERS

I thought people might like to hear the story of my son, Lee. It just might give hope to anyone going through a similar situation.

Six days after Lee's third birthday, I had to take him to see our doctor. Since the previous Christmas, he had had one minor illness after another. He was a very strange grey colour, and not interested in playing with his toys in the slightest.

He would just sit and stare into space all the time. On this visit to the doctor, he took a blood test. At six o'clock that evening, his car drew up outside our house, and we knew that there was something seriously wrong.

It was leukaemia which, to me, at that time, meant certain death. I have never felt so empty, helpless and completely destroyed. All I could think, staring at him

113

as I tucked him up in bed, was that this disease was going to take him away from me.

The next morning, my husband, Neil, and I took Lee to hospital. They took a small sample of his bone marrow, and more blood, and confirmed that it was leukaemia. The paediatrician explained that the treatment would consist of three years of chemotherapy, and a two-week course of radiotherapy. He had a curable type of the disease, and his chances of a complete recovery were fifty/fifty.

The initial treatment lasted for nearly two weeks in hospital. He had drugs injected daily, as well as blood tests and pills. After several weeks, he would willingly put his arm out for an injection, and would put anything up to twelve pills in his mouth, swallowing them down in one go.

At the start of the fifth week, he had to have radiotherapy on his head. His head had to be kept very, very still during the treatment. So he had to have this plastic mask made. This was put on him, then bolted to the table.

This was one of the worst parts of his treatment. But as usual, he didn't complain, or cry. He just accepted it as part of his treatment, as he did everything else. The only side-effect from his radiotherapy was that his remaining hair fell out. Six weeks later, he slept for almost a week, which was something we had been warned about.

He then went into remission. There were no leukaemia cells to be seen in his bone marrow. His treatment for the next three years consisted of daily pills, an injection once a month, a bone marrow test every three months, and blood tests three times a week.

We then settled into a fairly normal family life again. Lee's hair regrew, he lost the weight he had put on, and he looked and acted like any normal little boy. Things had been going well for a year, when he picked up a virus, which put him back in hospital. After a week, his blood count had improved, his temperature came down, and he was allowed home.

However, the following day, his temperature shot up again, and he had to be re-admitted. Up went the drip again, and in went the drugs. Septicaemia was diagnosed, and he had to spend another week in hospital.

Shortly after that episode, his hair fell out again. But Lee just didn't mind. He simply said that if he had no hair, he wouldn't have to wash it! I minded, though, having to put up with all the staring faces and the whispered comments when we went out together.

The second year of his treatment was the worst. He was in and out of hospital about six or seven times, with anything from a virus to a chest infection to shingles! He picked up a particularly nasty virus. For six weeks, he had a sickness bug, which he seemed unable to shake off. He lost over a stone again, and had to have two blood transfusions.

His blood count was so low, it was off the bottom of the chart. He had virtually no blood cells – red or white. We were told to treat him like a china doll – even a slight knock could start him haemorrhaging.

Then the doctor told us the really bad news. His last bone-marrow result was not good. It looked as though Lee was suffering a relapse – the leukaemia was coming back. As he was still receiving treatment, the outlook was very black.

All the old doubts and fears came back. Lee was not going to be one of the increasingly lucky ones who made it. He was sent back to hospital. The doctor told us that they would not be able to do another bone-marrow test to confirm the relapse for five days. Those five days seemed like five years.

The results, however, were the same as the previous

test. It was possible that the recent severe virus could have affected his bone marrow, or he could be in the early stages of a relapse.

His blood count started to improve, and he was sent home. He then had fortnightly bone-marrow tests, which gradually improved. He hadn't relapsed. Thirteen months later, his treatment was able to stop as suddenly as it started.

He has now been off the treatment for over two years. He is very healthy, a very normal eight-year-old boy. The treatment has left no scars, physically and mentally, and his chances of a complete cure are looking better all the time.

The last five years have not been easy for the family. Perhaps it has been worst for our daughter, Sharon. She was five years old when Lee was first diagnosed – old enough to realize that something was going on.

Friends always asked how Lee was, never her. She was bundled from place to place, so that I would be with Lee. If she was not at school, she had to come to the outpatients' department while he had his treatment. But she never showed any jealousy or resentment at all. Even though her brother was not able to go to any of the places where other children were – the zoo, the park, the seaside – neither of them ever complained.

I would like my 'Our Tune' dedicated to a wonderful family who have never once complained when one little brave boy was going through so much.

CHAPTER SIX

Marriage . . . and Affairs

Maggie

'*Maggie's story shows the other side of an affair, and, perhaps, just how some people never change.*'
[BROADCAST: AUGUST 1987]

*I hold on to your body and feel each
move you make
Your voice is warm and tender
A love that I could not forsake*
'THE POWER OF LOVE'–JENNIFER RUSH

In early 1980, I started a new job near my home in Liverpool. There was no special person in my life, as I was kept busy with my three kids from my previous marriage. I had my own little house, and I was quite content with life.

Through my new job, I came into contact with James. We became friends, and started having the odd lunch together. Over a few months, he told me of his unhappy marriage. He had no kids, and he told me that his marriage was really a relationship in name only. Slowly, but surely, an affair started.

And, just as surely, I fell in love with him, and he with me. During the summer of that year, he decided he wanted to leave his wife, and to come and live with me in my house. That summer, his wife went on holiday. And it was during that time that he moved out of his house and into mine.

Imagine the anguish of his wife when she came back to find him gone. As it turned out, it was a complete shock to her, as there was absolutely nothing wrong with their marriage as far as she knew. She hadn't wanted to have children for a while, and that was the reason they hadn't tried for a family.

Anyway, we sold my little house, and bought an old cottage in the country. After a while, she found us, and started to come around. She cried, begging him to return to her.

During all of this, I discovered I was pregnant. James was over the moon. He said he would make a wonderful dad, and take care of me, my kids and our new arrival for the rest of our lives.

His divorce came through, just as little Nicola was born. We didn't have much money, but we were madly in love, and oh, so happy.

I went back to work to help out, and for five years everything was rosy. James got promotion, and my wages became extra for holidays and all those little perks. Then we went to Portugal on holiday, and had a fantastic time. We we so happy that James suggested that on our next wedding anniversary we should have a church service to bless us.

A few months later, I started to notice a change in him. He started coming home later; he wasn't so interested in me; he stayed away a few nights for work. He had cooled off, and I didn't know why. I pleaded, begged, cried, and nearly drove myself to a nervous breakdown, but he never gave any sort of explanation about why he had started to turn so cold.

From October to February, I struggled to keep him happy. In all this, little Nicola, who loved her daddy so much, couldn't understand what was going on. She had never known us have any rows before.

During the next half-term holiday, I decided to go with Nicola to visit my parents. We had a lovely week, and finally got home on the Saturday evening. What greeted us was a scene straight out of my worst nightmare. All of James's belongings, passport, cameras,

papers – everything – had gone. He'd done it again –
a flit in the middle of the night.

My daughter, my kids and I went to pieces. It was
awful, as you can imagine. Well, he never came back.
A new girl had started at his firm that Autumn, and an
affair had started. It was an exact carbon copy of what
had happened before.

The only difference this time was that he had a won-
derful daughter to cherish and protect. He was very
cruel. We never knew where he went, and still don't
know where he lives. He picks up Nicola once a month,
and that's the only time we ever see him.

I am now divorced, and I suppose he is starting on
marriage number three. I have lost all confidence in
men. I am only here today because of my daughter, and
some great supportive friends.

I can't believe that I even knew the man that I loved
so much. After he left, I discovered all sorts of debts he
owed. He gave us no help at all. I only wish I could
turn the clock back, before I met him, when I was happy
and content with my lot. The only good thing is that I
have Nicola. She is my world, but it is so sad that she
has to go through all this.

What gives anyone the right to just abandon a family
when a new face enters their life? Now I know exactly
what his first wife went through. All I can say is that I
am really sorry wherever you are.

The song that used to sum up my feelings for him is
'The Power of Love', by Jennifer Rush. From tomorrow,
I start a new phase in my life. I am no longer madly in
love with him, but I suppose a small part of me will
always be with him.

I can feel strong now to face up to a future alone.
Life has to go on, doesn't it?

Andrea

'Andrea's story is a classic case of an affair that seemed so good, and so romantic, that she wanted to sacrifice everything for it, including Dave, her husband who loved her. Eventually, it all went terribly wrong – for everyone. But hers is also a story of hope, and how couples can sometimes find strengths in each other that they never knew were there.'

[BROADCAST: DECEMBER 1988]

> *Whenever this world is cruel to me*
> *I've got you, you're all I need*
> *You are making me live, you're my*
> *best friend*
> 'YOU'RE MY BEST FRIEND'–QUEEN

I may be five years too late writing to you, Simon, but this record sums up what Dave means to me. Maybe it means as much, or even more, today than it did then. It all started nearly seven years ago, when my children had both started school and I went back to work. I started as a part-time typist, and I liked Steve, the manager, the first time I saw him. We quickly became friends.

When I had been there a short time, it became obvious that because the way the company was expanding, another manager was needed. Steve began teaching me about the job. I wasn't bright or quick, but he laboured on, and taught me everything I needed to know.

When the big bosses noticed how well we worked together, they decided it would be a good idea to send me to college to get my management qualification. They thought it would also be a good idea if Steve came along as well, to help me and act as a refresher course for him.

I had been nothing but a wife and mother for over six years, and although I'd loved being with my children, and each of their milestones in their lives made me the happiest mum in the world, the sort of challenge this exam gave me filled the gap they left better than I ever could have imagined.

I employed a child minder, and Dave and I worked out a system that whoever got home first would look after the children. Because of all the overtime I was working, I had taken to popping into the pub with the others for a well-earned drink. Dave wasn't very thrilled with this arrangement, but I tried hard to make it up to him.

After two months, the evening classes were over, and Steve and I had become very close. He worked hard to help me pass the exam, and I was very grateful. It seemed only natural that we should give each other a little peck on the cheek.

One night, after a party, Steve and I found ourselves alone. I was pretty naïve and tipsy. You know what happened. I was racked with guilt, and we both swore it would never happen again. We cooled off for a while, but one night it all started again. We did all the things that people said were romantic, but I had never believed.

Walking barefoot on the beach on a moonlit summer night, taking the dogs for long walks through the woods while we picked blackberries in the rain, drying out in front of a blazing log fire. It was unreal, but it was happening to me. Everything was rose coloured and beautiful.

When Dave and I talked, it was all spiteful and full of recriminations. Eventually, he took my advice and moved in with his parents to give me a chance to sort myself out. Steve would come over in the evenings while the kids were in bed, and would sneak out again in the morning.

Eventually the strain became too much, and we came to the conclusion that we had to be together all of the time. I packed myself up and moved in with Steve. Dave, as you can imagine, was devastated, but I hardened myself, and in my own selfish way tried to be fair to him. I didn't take any money for myself, and gave him open-ended access to the kids. Big of me!

My family broke into factions – for and against, mostly against. Work became impossible. I was losing credibility, just being thought of as Steve's bit of stuff. It rubbed off on him, so we decided that I should leave. Being at home with nothing to occupy me, I ran out of things to laugh at.

My mum would often come round and get stuck into the backlog of housework and washing that I now always seemed to have. But when Dave started seeing my sister Tracy, it brought about such a storm in our family, and it made me crumble into a nervous wreck.

Steve was a bewildered onlooker. Although he tried, he didn't have a clue what to do; so, in the end, he left me to sort it out. At this point, my mum took over, and saved our lives and our world. She took me to the doctor, but he just told me to 'pull myself together'. So my mum began a reconciliation between me and Dave. She would come with me when I dropped the kids off for their time with Dave, and then borrow the car for a quick bit of shopping, forcing us to make conversation.

On Mother's Day morning, just over a year after Dave had gone to stay with his parents, I came home. There were no trumpets, no fanfares, and things weren't right for a very long time, but the cure had started as soon as I walked through the door. Dave got back a very different family from the one that had left.

But, instead of thinking he was a lily-livered wimp, I began to see strengths in Dave that I never knew he had. He shared himself with me and the kids, until we were able to start thinking for ourselves again.

I don't know if I am a better person for what happened, but it showed me what friends really are, and it showed me that Dave is the best I've got.

Tessa

'For Tessa, from Liverpool, her affair had an altogether different ending. Sadly, four people's lives became hopelessly tangled. Three managed to find happiness, but for Tessa it was another story.'

[BROADCAST: APRIL 1988]

> *People can change*
> *They often do*
> *Haven't you noticed the changes in you*
> 'BEING WITH YOU'–SMOKEY ROBINSON

I hope writing this letter will help me understand and cope with the situation I have found myself in. My name is Tessa, and I'm forty years old. I was married to Ben – a really good man – for five years. But in September last year, our marriage was in a bit of a rut.

124

Ben is a long-distance lorry driver, and I was bored and lonely.

Ben's brother-in-law, Dave, used to come to my house. His marriage was stormy from time to time, and I guess at the time we were both needing company and affection.

We didn't mean it to happen, but we fell in love.

We lived for each moment we could spend together. It wasn't the usual jump-into-bed affair. If it had been, perhaps things would have been different now. At first we were very careful not to be found out, but as we got more and more involved with each other, we began to take chances: having lunch, walking in the town together.

As Christmas approached, we exchanged gifts and cards. I still have my gift, and treasure it very much. I was even foolish enough to keep his card at home. I didn't care, you see. I was so in love, making plans in my mind for the future.

A few days after Christmas, it happened. Ben found the card. He knew at once who it was from, although I denied it. After a lot of shouting and arguing, I left the house and managed to get a message to Dave.

We met, and we talked, and decided to leave town together, with just the clothes we were wearing. We pooled our money, filled the car with petrol, and headed to some friends down south. It was hard for us, but we were happy and so in love. Ben managed to trace us, and there were phone calls and meetings. But we stuck to our guns to stay together.

Then, late one night, there was a phone call to say Ben was in hospital. He had taken an overdose. Dave and I travelled through the night, and arrived at the hospital early in the morning, both afraid of what we would find.

I still cared about Ben, and didn't want anything to

happen to him. Once we were back, though, everyone seemed to think we had come back to be with our partners. Our families pushed us hard, too hard – so hard, in fact, that we had to go away again.

Dave and I found somewhere locally to live. The next few weeks were very traumatic – all my emotions were mixed up and confused, and there was terrible pressure on both of us. It was all too much for Dave, who tried to go back to his wife. But within a few days, we had drifted back into an affair again, with him spending as much time as he could at our house.

Ten days later, he came back, but, I can see now, for all the wrong reasons.

By now, Ben had found another woman, and moved in with her. I was deeply hurt. He had promised to let me have time to sort myself out, and I felt he had broken that promise – that he didn't really love me.

Thinking about it now, of course, I realize I had no right at all to feel that way. After all, he was just trying to pick up the pieces of his life again. It was me who had left him. Ben had taken most of our possessions, and what he did leave me had to go back to pay outstanding bills.

It just didn't work out at all with Dave, and now, here I am in an empty old house, with just a few pieces of second-hand furniture – no money for the bills, no job and no one I can turn to for help.

There is really only Ben, if I could pluck up the courage to ask him to help me. I still care about him very much. I miss him, and wonder what he is doing, how he is getting along.

I think he is all right. I think Dave is OK too, back with his wife. We were just four ordinary people who had become hopelessly and sadly involved. Three of them have survived – only one of them not sure whether she will.

I want my tune dedicated to Ben. It was 'Our Tune' in 1981, when we first met: 'Being with You', by Smokey Robinson.

PS: I didn't need to find the courage to contact Ben in the end. Wonderful man that he is, he came to see me as soon as he heard what had happened. We talked, and are going to get divorced. But Ben says he will always be there if I need help. I want to thank him for that. I still love him, and I always will.

Robin

'It's strange sometimes how you never know what you've got until it's gone. Robin's letter shows you what I mean.'

[BROADCAST: DECEMBER 1988]

> How can it be that a love carved out
>   of caring
> Fashioned by faith would suffer so hard
> From the games played once too often
> 'SOMETHING ABOUT YOU'–LEVEL 42

Although I got engaged to a lovely girl called Jane, things started to go wrong almost straightaway. She was very possessive, and I couldn't handle that.

One evening I went out for a drink at the local wine bar with a few friends. There, I met a girl called Sarah. She was seventeen, I was twenty-one. She made me laugh, and was good company. I was a little selfish, and poured out my heart to her. Sarah was very understanding. I asked her out for a drink, but she said no, because I was committed, already being engaged.

Two weeks later, I saw her again, and we chatted and enjoyed each other's company. I told her that the engagement was off, and that Jane and I felt we could not cope with the situation. I asked Sarah out for a drink, and this time she said yes. Two weeks after the engagement was broken off, Jane announced to everyone in the pub that she was pregnant. I was speechless, and Sarah, understandably, was very upset.

I talked seriously and at length with Jane, and told her that it was still all over. I know this was the wrong way to handle the situation, but it was how I felt at the time. Sarah and I talked through the night, and decided to give our friendship and company the chance to grow into a serious relationship. For five months, we were inseparable, not just a couple, but good friends as well.

People were beginning to see Sarah and I as an item. Then, in December, just four weeks before the baby was due to be born, Sarah began to get strange feelings. She felt that I wanted Jane and the baby. She became slightly paranoid.

We argued, but then always kissed and made up. We always seemed to need each other more afterwards. I can understand how Sarah must have felt. Then Jane had her baby. I began to think more and more about my responsibilities, and the situation became too much for both of us. Sarah told me that I must talk to Jane, to sort out our problems and our differences.

She told me that she loved me, but for her own peace of mind, it was something she felt we both had to do. The last kiss with Sarah was something I shall never forget. I went to see Jane, and we decided that for the sake of the baby, we would try again.

We moved in together, and in August of this year, we married. We really did it for the sake of our child, and I am in a marriage where I have to learn to love my wife.

But I feel that in the last year, I have grown up from a big kid into a responsible husband and father. I know Sarah is now somewhere in London, and I just want to say a big thank you to her for helping to open my eyes, a thank you for helping me grow up, and, most of all, a thank you for the times we shared together.

I feel I have hurt Jane enough, but I know we can make a go of everything. There really is something about her that I've grown to love.

Vera

'I get so many letters from people who have become tangled in affairs, only to see it end in tears. Vera from Halifax told me one such story.'

[BROADCAST: JANUARY 1988]

> Because I'm truly
> Truly in love with you girl
> I'm truly head over heels with your love
> 'TRULY'–LIONEL RICHIE

It is so difficult to write everything down, and make it seem exactly how it was, but I will try. In the Autumn of 1982, I met Malcolm. I was nineteen, and he was thirty-seven, and married. I knew right from the start that he was married, but as I was young and naïve, I didn't care.

I think I was only looking for fun – until I fell in love. He felt the same about me, and he was the first to say it. I have never felt anything like it before. I was so happy.

I was working as a nanny, and was alone all day with the little boy I looked after. Malcolm started calling me three times a day, and I came to depend on the calls. He was very loving. He constantly bought me presents – just small things on the spur of the moment, but they meant everything to me.

We met as often as we could. Everytime he had any spare time we saw each other. Even on a Sunday, when he was supposed to be out buying a newspaper, he would phone me, and spend some minutes with me. I had had a really terrible childhood. My stepfather had been really strict with me, and my mum couldn't seem to help me. When Malcolm came along, perhaps I was looking for a father figure. But all I knew was that I eventually loved him.

Six months after it all started, he told me the affair was all over. He said he couldn't carry on, becuase it wasn't fair to his wife. I cried all day and night. My mum, who I love dearly, was very supportive, but I was heartbroken. I hated the pain I was feeling. I couldn't imagine life without him.

I didn't know how I would cope at work without his three phone calls a day. The next morning, at nine o'clock – an hour earlier than he usually called – he phoned me. He said he was sorry, and that he had to keep seeing me. He loved me, and he couldn't go through with it.

I was so happy, but my mum was furious. She could see exactly what was happening. We carried on for another twelve months. Our love was totally consuming. We spent every moment together, holding each other, walking, talking, loving.

I lived from one telephone call to the next. But, very slowly, I began to realize that there was no future in it.

Through my job, I met Ray. I didn't love him at all like I loved Malcolm. But, at last, I could do 'normal' things, like going to the pub together, parties, the cinema – all without any secrecy.

I still saw Malcolm, but he wasn't my whole life anymore. The following year, I went to work in a local government office. I had only been there for three weeks when Malcolm suddenly phoned. His wife had found out about us, and he couldn't see me anymore. But, because I had now found someone else in my life, it was easier to take.

It was still very, very painful. I missed him so much, everything seemed to remind me of him. But, gradually, as the months went by, he turned into a lovely memory. I went to work in America for a year, and when I came back, I decided to look him up. It was really just a call to an 'old friend'. I phoned him at work, but he wasn't there.

I don't know why, but I panicked because he wasn't where I had always pictured him. I got my brother to phone his home, and leave a message for him to call me. He called, and was very, very angry. He told me to leave him alone, not to phone. Yes, he still thought about me – that would never change. But he said he had taken forever to rebuild his life.

I was very upset. He had never spoken to me like that. But I realized how selfish I had been. I had managed to get over him, while he had suffered turmoil and upset with his wife. A couple of months later, I saw his car, and found out where he was working. It was an accident – I hadn't meant or tried to find him. I saw him that evening – he was surprised to see me.

We had a chat. That's all I meant to do. It was difficult: me at one side of the car, him as far away as possible at the other. How do you say everything that's happened over three years in twenty minutes? How can you be cool when you have loved someone so much?

I didn't realize I still loved him until I saw him, but it was my mistake. In the end, he admitted he still loved me. I thought constantly about him again. Although I was trying hard to get him out of my mind, we met twice more. It wasn't like before, but our feelings were still there.

Then, one day, his wife phoned me. I felt cold inside – so completely guilty. This time it was my fault. Before it had been Malcolm's fault as well, but this time it was really all my doing.

I told his wife that I hadn't seen Malcolm at all. I said he had told me to go away, and that he didn't want to see me. I don't know whether she believed me or not, but it seemed to calm her down. I saw him just once more. He didn't want to see me. We just said goodbye. I feel horrible.

I'm so frightened that I'll never love anyone like him again. I will always love him; he has said there will always be a very special place in his heart for me. But I still feel guilty. I know he was trying hard not to see me. I probably seem very selfish. I suppose I am.

I don't know why I ever tried to see him again, but I can't go back now. I will probably go abroad to work – run away from it all yet again.

When I first knew Malcolm, he bought me 'Truly', by Lionel Richie. That was our song, and the song that really sums up everything I ever felt about him.

Jake

'And, of course, it is also men who can suffer in affairs. Jake wrote to me from Dorset with his experience.'
[BROADCAST: DECEMBER 1987]

> *A love like ours is love that is hard to find*
> *How could we let it slip away*
> *When tomorrow comes and we both regret the things we said today*
> 'IF YOU LEAVE ME NOW'–CHICAGO

I am sitting here wondering how I am going to face my thirty-second birthday alone. Until just a few months ago, I had a wonderful wife and two children.

However, as the result of a relationship with a very close friend of my wife's – which lasted three weeks – my wife decided she could no longer live with me. It was up to me then to make every effort towards a reconciliation. As I now realize, there is no pain like unrequited love, for it seems the harder I try to make amends, my pleas and promises seem to fall on deaf ears.

My own family has never been really close, so in many ways I have never had anyone with whom I could talk it through. The only relief in all this mess has been the visits of my two wonderful children. They brought my house to life and made it feel like a home again.

But, throughout this time, my wife has been consulting a solicitor, a step I refuse to take – simply because I did not and still do not want a divorce. I realize that by having an affair, I completely destroyed the faith my wife had in me. But the torment it has put me through is incredible.

I had to take time off work through depression. I tried to commit suicide by taking in one go all the anti-depressant pills I had been prescribed. But, at the last minute, I could not take the coward's way out and commit suicide. I was taken to hospital and recovered. It may have been a plea to my wife to come back to me, but again, I failed miserably.

The suicide attempt only served to convince her that I was not the sort of fit, responsible husband she wanted. I sought psychiatric help, and I moved in with my sister, in an effort to find some happiness away from a house of memories. But the damage I have caused to my wife, children and family is so enormous, I sometimes think I cannot cope any more.

I have decided that I must get back on my feet, and try to show my wife that I am a capable father, and capable as a husband. But believe me, it is impossible to be positive when my wife and family are no longer around.

I have managed to discuss with my wife reasonable access to the children – one day a week. I do tend to go overboard with them, and that doesn't meet with my wife's approval. But at least we are a little more tolerant of each other. I know that my wife is level-headed, and will eventually decide if we have enough upon which to build a future together.

I hope that in time, I will give my wife enough reason to start to trust me again. I want my letter to serve as a warning. I allowed myself to stray from my family, and my wife decided that if we did not have trust between us, we really had nothing.

I don't want anyone else in my life. I hope my wife will eventually realize this. But I know, having had an affair with someone else, it is difficult for her. One day, I hope I can convince her.

CHAPTER SEVEN
Suicide

Alison

'So often it is easy to give up, think every relationship you are ever likely to have is going to end in nothing but tears – or tragedy. So many letters come to me from people who have reached such depths of despair, all they want to do is end it. Twice, I have had to talk someone out of suicide on the air. But all too often, something happens, and you realize there is that special person out there.

   Alison told me how she almost gave up, before she found true happiness.'

[BROADCAST: FEBRUARY 1989]

> I want to know what love is
> I want you to show me
> I want to feel what love is
> > 'I WANT TO KNOW WHAT LOVE IS'
> > –FOREIGNER

I had a fairly average and happy childhood. I liked school, and had several friends. I began seeing boys when I was sixteen, and had some good times, but nothing serious. In 1985, I took my O-levels, and passed all but one. Then I began taking my A-level course. It started all right, then got steadily worse. I found I couldn't cope with the maths or chemistry, and began to get worried. I approached my teachers about it, and they told me it would be all right in the end, so I just carried on.

I took my mock A-levels, failed them, and got seriously worried again. I got steadily more and more worried as time went on, and blew things out of all proportion. My A-levels were important, but not so important that what happened should have occurred – I tried to take my life with an overdose of aspirin.

I went to some wasteland near my home in Watford, and just took the tablets. I lay down and waited to fall asleep. Then, for some reason, I changed my mind, and staggered back to the road. I found a phone box and called an ambulance. They managed to get me to hospital, where my stomach was pumped.

A nurse asked if I wanted to see my parents. I decided I did, and they were called. I was in for four days, my mum coming to see me at every opportunity. She was really great.

Looking back, I don't think it was the A-levels that caused the depression. They started it all off, but I think it was a lack of communication that made me try to commit suicide. I've never been able to talk to anyone about any problems I'd been having. I'd just bottle up things inside, until they blew up.

Then, in March 1987, I met 'the bloke'. His name was Joe – he was six years older than me, and basically knocked me off my feet. He cared about me, and I fell hook, line and sinker. I found I could talk to him, confide in him, and he was always there if I needed just a cuddle.

Things were great for about ten months, then they began to go wrong. I don't know what happened, but he ended up finishing with me. It was all very sudden and I took it very badly. I was upset and very depressed for a couple of months. He started seeing someone else, which really hurt me.

I used to spend most of my time avoiding him, but when I was really depressed, would go to see him. At the beginning of May, we sorted things out a bit. We were more relaxed with each other, and I didn't feel so bitter.

One evening, we were due to meet at a local club. I turned up at nine o'clock, and asked for him at reception. The girl behind the desk asked me to wait a minute, then went to find the manager. He told me to come to his office.

He sat me down, and exactly what he said I can't remember. But he explained that the police had found a body on a nearby railway line. It seemed as though Joe had fallen from a bridge. For more than a week, I was in a complete daze.

My mother was great. She tried to help me get over it, because I was due to re-sit my A-levels three weeks later. I think I got over it reasonably well, but it still really hurts. I suppose it's something you never really recover from.

I coped as well as I could, and when I got my A-level results, I had done reasonably well. I was accepted at Durham University, where I found everyone really friendly and easy to get on with.

I saw a guy for a couple of months, but it didn't really work out. One Wednesday, I was feeling depressed and sorry for myself, and managed to get drunk in the middle of the afternoon to put it out of my mind. It was something I had sworn I would never do. That was when Mike found me. It took him ages to get anything out of me, but for some unknown reason, I suddenly told him everything.

The next few days were great, and things have gone from good to better. I have never felt this way before about anybody. I found I love Mike and always will. We were both heartbroken when we had to go home at Christmas, and couldn't wait until we got to see each other again.

I suddenly realized how many people do actually love you, and really care about you. If you are alone, and depressed and think about suicide, it is just not worth it.

If you are looking for love, don't look too hard. You'll be surprised how close love can be.

Mary

'Mary also thought about committing suicide, driven to it by a terrible relationship and a very unhappy home life. But, to paraphrase the movies, she didn't get even, she got mad!'

[BROADCAST: MARCH 1989]

> *And I won't be the one who'll come*
> *running*
> *It ain't like it used to be*
> *It's your turn to run to me*
> 'NO MORE THE FOOL'–ELKIE BROOKS

Ever since I was young, I have always been looking for love. My father has never kissed or cuddled me, or showed me any attention at all, except to tell me how he couldn't wait for me to leave, so he would never have to set eyes on me again.

My mother is lovely, but totally dominated by my father, who regularly gets very violent towards me – and to her, if she tries to help.

My young brother has grown up in this environment,

141

and he thinks that it is normal to act in this way. Now he is taller and stronger than me, he acts in exactly the same manner. Surprisingly, it is the things they say that hurt more than the things they do to me. But I understand that this is the way that they are, and that they will never change.

When I was eighteen, I prepared to leave home, but my mum begged and cried for me to stay. The only person in my family who I have been able to turn to is my auntie, but she has been fighting cancer for four years. So instead of her being there for me, I have to be there for her. She has enough to contend with, without my problems as well.

At the end of 1984, Christmas time to be exact, I met a man called Bill. We seemed perfectly matched. In fact, I remember saying at the time that it seemed too good to be true. I guess you could say that I had finally found what I was looking for.

We spent every free minute we had together. I was so happy. Things at home eased off; my family adored Bill, and he seemed to like them too. What could go wrong?

In August 1986, my father changed his job, and the family moved to Kent. Bill said this wouldn't change anything and, true to his word, he wrote and phoned every week. I was so happy at that time, planning for the time we would be together again – for two weeks at Christmas.

But on Christmas Eve, he phoned and told me he was planning an engagement party – *his*!

I was devastated. I had only got a letter from him three days before, telling me how much he loved me, and missed me, and how he was counting the days until we were together again. I spent the whole of Christmas in my room, trying to come to terms with it all. My world was absolutely shattered.

Somehow, I managed to get through it all. Then, in April, the letters and the phone calls began coming again. Bill told me it had all been a terrible mistake. Fool that I was, I took him back.

It's hard to explain why. My only excuse is that I really did love him. Things went back to normal, and the upset of that Christmas was put behind us. I hadn't yet told Bill of a holiday in Spain I had booked with some girls from work. I was going to an eighteen/thirty resort, and I knew how jealous Bill could get (ironic, really, after the things he gets up to).

But, the holiday was booked, and I was going to go. At the end of June, Bill and I had a fantastic two weeks together. To say I was over the moon was an understatement. At the end of that time, I told Bill about the holiday. He was furious!

He told me not to go. I managed to convince him that it would be all right, but he wasn't happy about it at all. I went, and it was a really welcome break in the sun. The other girls met loads of blokes, but I wasn't interested. I just wanted to get back to see Bill again.

A week after I got back from holiday, I suffered a miscarriage. I hadn't even known I was pregnant. Bill phoned on the same day, and mum told him the news. I spoke to him a couple of days later, and he said that going on holiday had killed our baby. He called me a murderess, and said that he would never forgive me.

My family said that I deserved everything I got, that I could expect no sympathy from them. They even banned me from mentioning the subject again. I was so full of guilt and depression. I had lost everything. I was all alone. I had nobody to talk to. No close friends. No one –

I know that I will sound weak and stupid to some people, but I got more and more depressed. I left my job because I couldn't bear to face people. I started drinking – a little at first, then drinking to forget.

Christmas 1986 was a blur. I had met Bill at Christmas, the previous Christmas he had got engaged, and this Christmas I was all alone. Many a time, I felt so bad, I only wanted to commit suicide.

On Christmas Eve, I cut my wrist. Accidentally, I said. But if I was a murderess, didn't I deserve to die?

In May 1987, I received a letter from a friend, telling me that Bill had got married the week before. This was only eight months after he had left me, eight months after my miscarriage.

At first I was upset. I cried a lot. Then I started to get really angry. How quickly they forget. I realized that no matter how much I loved him, he wasn't worth all the pain I had put myself through.

I then started to try to pull myself together. I cut down on the drinking, got a new job, and started to realize that, after all, maybe life isn't all that bad. I don't drink at all now. No matter what life throws at me, I think I can cope. I've come through this a stronger person. I realize now that I didn't kill my baby; it was just one of those things that happen.

Things aren't perfect, but then, when in this life are they? I'm not ready for another relationship yet, but in time who knows?

To anybody out there who feels like the world is coming to an end, or they are all alone with nobody to turn to – don't give up, because things really do get better.

Ironically, I've just received a gigantic Christmas card from Bill. On top of that, the phone calls and the letters have started to come again. Apparently, he's made another mistake!

But this time, he hasn't got me to fall back on. I've

refused to take him back. Now, more than ever, my tune, 'No More the Fool', seems the perfect one for me.

CHAPTER EIGHT
Torn Emotions

Paul

'Of all the emotions, jealousy is the one that can drive people to the greatest excesses. This letter, from Paul in Halifax, shows just what I mean.'

[BROADCAST: JANUARY 1985]

> *I hope you don't mind that I put down*
> *in words*
> *How wonderful life is*
> *While you're in this world*

'YOUR SONG'–ELTON JOHN

I don't really know where to begin my story, Simes, but I know that I have completely ruined everything I had by losing the girl I truly loved.

It began back in 1982, when I moved to the London area from Lancashire. I was working here as a computer programmer. I didn't have any friends in the area but, thankfully, the people I worked with took me under their wing.

One of the secretaries that worked for my company was a beautiful girl called Sue. She was blonde, intelligent and, having just come back from Corfu, incredibly suntanned. All the guys I worked with could see from the very first moment that I fancied her, and I think she suspected as much as well.

I had a bit of a problem. I know it sounds like an old cliché, but when you come from the North you are always very worried that people in the South will dismiss you – you know, as being from the old flat-cap brigade.

I didn't really have the enormous amount of confidence I would have needed to go up to her and ask her out. I think she realized this, and on one Friday evening, when the people from work invited me to the wine bar for a drink, she asked me if I was busy over the weekend.

You see, she had no fears at all! I told her that I had no plans (living in a bedsit outside town, I didn't have anything to do at all). She told me she was having a party at her home in Twickenham, and would I like to go?

I couldn't begin to tell you how excited I was. But I think in my own mind, I blew the invitation out of all proportion. It wasn't really a personal invitation – when I arrived on the Saturday evening, there were eighty people at her flat.

I felt really out of it. I didn't know anybody, and Sue seemed far too busy to make sure I was being looked after. I only stayed for about three or four drinks, and went home.

Incredibly, on Monday morning, Sue asked me why I had left so early. I made some lame excuse about being tired. She said that she was sorry she had not had a chance to talk to me because she wanted the party to be a success – but she had really looked forward to my being there.

For one of the first times in my life, I plucked up the courage to take the initiative. To make up for leaving early, I said that I would take her to see a film in the West End. Sue agreed, and we had a great night. I don't want this to sound like I was a lovestruck kind of teenager, but I have to say, I really thought she was great – with every attribute I had ever wanted to find in a girl.

After the film, we had a meal, and spent the night chatting and laughing. We had a lot of mutual interests, and made a few more dates to see each other. Within a few weeks, we had become a couple. It was really great. Sue agreed to come and stay at my little place at the weekend, and even helped me decorate and furnish it.

And, during the week, I would spend a few nights at her flat. Our relationship seemed perfect, and I can honestly say that I have never been so happy in my life.

But the first signs of a problem came a few months later. We had gone out to a party organized by another secretary from work. It was the first time we had been in a big group of other people socially.

All our previous dates had been quiet ones – a movie, a meal at an Indian restaurant, a drive out to the country. But at the party, there was everyone from work, and a whole load of people I had never seen before.

I wasn't driving that night, so I had quite a bit to drink. Sue had a few glasses of wine as well. I spent some time in the kitchen, talking to a guy from work, and didn't see Sue for about half an hour.

When I went into the lounge, everyone was dancing. It was a slow song, and there was Sue in the middle of the crowd, dancing cheek to cheek with a guy I had never seen before. I felt myself grow more and more angry. I must have been standing on the side of the room for about fifteen minutes. When Sue came over to me, she pretended nothing had happened.

I asked her to get her coat, so we could go. Although she was surprised, she came with me. Outside, I told her how angry I was. We had a furious row. She told me that she had been dancing with a load of other guys while I had been talking in the kitchen, and that she would dance with anyone she wanted to when we went to a party.

You see, Simon, I discovered that I thought so much of Sue, I couldn't stand seeing her with anyone else. And as the months went on, the feelings got worse and worse. We went out to lots of places together, and Sue, being an outgoing girl, would always be the life and soul of the party. I couldn't stand it. I was so jealous.

A lot of it had to do with the fact that I was a shy person, myself, and she was so different to me in public. After every party we went to, there would always be a row. It was terrible. In the end, Sue warned me that she would bring our relationship to an end if I didn't grow up.

But it all came to a head when we went to our office Christmas party. We managed to have a few dances together, but Sue managed to dance with almost everyone in the disco.

I got really drunk. In the toilets, I told one of my friends that Sue was making a complete and total fool of me. He told me to grow up and not to be stupid. But the more I drank, the more depressed and angry I became. When Sue came back to the bar, I grabbed her, and we had the most terrible row.

I told her she was coming home with me, but she refused. I told her that if she loved me, she would stop dancing with everybody else in the room. In fairness, she tried to quieten me down, and make me see reason. But I got louder and louder, until in the end she stormed off.

I waited for hours outside her flat, and when she came home, we had the most terrible row. She told me that if I couldn't let her enjoy her life, she didn't want to see me. I told her that it suited me.

But I had embarrassed her so much, she finished our

relationship. Why did I get so possessive and jealous? I can't believe that I have destroyed a love affair that was so good. Perhaps one day I will be able to control this jealousy.

I honestly don't think that I stand any chance of winning Sue back. She has left our company, but I think she really is too outgoing for me, and I don't think I would ever be able to control my feelings when we were out together.

But 'Your Song' was a song that was very special to us at the beginning. I think about her every time I hear it. If nothing else comes out of this, Simon, at least I have learned a very, very important lesson in life. You can never try to totally control someone else – especially if you really love them.

Michael

'There is nothing worse than truly not knowing what you want in life. And if you can't make a decision, then you could end up a loser all round. Michael has found that out the hard way.'

[BROADCAST: JANUARY 1989]

> *When the river was deep, I didn't falter*
> *When the mountain was high, I still*
> *   believed*
> *When the valley was low, it didn't*
> *   stop me,*
> *I knew you were waiting*
> > 'I KNEW YOU WERE WAITING'
> > –ARETHRA FRANKLIN AND GEORGE MICHAEL

I cannot believe that I am in the situation in which I have ended up. Just three years ago, I had the love of a really wonderful girl. I tried to give her up for someone else, who I loved just as much, and tragically fell between two stools.

I think I have probably lost everything now. I have never been able to talk honestly to either of the two girls about what happened – just by writing this I feel as though I have managed to unburden myself.

I used to live abroad, with a very kind, attractive, understanding, considerate and totally committed girl called Jody. We have been in the States for several years, and built up a nice life together. In the mid-1980s, I was transferred back to England with my job. That was the first problem.

My work took me around the world, and I literally spent thirteen hours a day at my office. I had a home, which I never saw, and a relationship which grew more and more empty because I couldn't put anything into it.

The cracks in our relationship began to show. She found herself a great job, and spent more and more time involving herself in work. Inevitably, although I was too blind to see it, she was becoming more and more involved with one of her colleagues.

It seemed all our friends realized that an affair was starting, but because I was so selfish, blind and wrapped up in my own work, I didn't recognize the warning signs.

Because I was devoting more and more time to the office – and doing quite well in my career – I found myself becoming closer and closer to one of the very pretty, intelligent executives.

Rachel and I started spending more and more time together. We had a close link with our job, and I genuinely seemed to make her laugh. Within a few months the second part of this sad jigsaw slotted into place, and we began an affair.

Rachel, however, was in a difficult position. She had a young son, Christian, even though she wasn't married. She had been close to Christian's father, but they had had problems in their relationship, and were living apart.

Our relationship just took off. It was total passion to begin with; then, I have to admit, against all the odds, it settled into something deeper. I had moved out of the house where I lived with Jody, and bought a flat of my own. But, this is where the most destructive element of all came into play.

I could never reconcile simply turning my back on someone I had loved and cherished for so many years to start a new relationship. And that stopped me making the ultimate commitment which Rachel and Christian so desperately wanted.

What could I do? For months I was in torment. I felt like I was literally being pulled in half. People said that I had a kind streak, and that streak simply wouldn't allow me to see anyone hurt. But my indecision was hurting everyone.

On several occasions, I tried desperately to force myself to make a commitment one way or the other. And every time, I felt blocked by being torn back towards the other relationship.

Don't get me wrong. I'm no film star. Just a normal guy, but hopelessly trapped in the middle of something I couldn't handle. But you also have to remember that, on one hand, my entire social life and friendships were built with Jody. On the other hand, a relationship that was filled with passion pulled me in the other direction.

It was no exaggeration to say this went on for over a year. And finally, the thing that I had been petrified of happening actually took place. Rachel, who had to think of Christian's security, decided she had to make a go of her relationship with his father. And Jody, who deserved and needed someone totally committed to her, found someone new.

I tried to be there for both of them, Simon. It proved impossible. Sometimes in life, you have to make a hard decision. If you sit on the fence, you could lose out all round.

'I Knew You Were Waiting' was so special to Rachel and me, because it summed up what I tried to do. Even though it hurts me everytime I hear it, it still has a deep place in my heart.

Patsy and Graham

'Patsy and Graham's story, from Solihull in the West Midlands, was one of the most stirring love stories I have ever read out. It also brought dozens of letters of support from other listeners.'

[BROADCAST: MAY 1987]

> I can see a new horizon
> Underneath a blazing sky
> I'll be where the eagles are flying
>   higher and higher
> 'ST ELMO'S FIRE'–JOHN PARR

This is honestly a love story which I should never really be writing. When I first set eyes on Graham, there seemed no chance at all that we would ever be together.

But, after three years, we are not only the happiest couple alive, but we are planning to marry in the next six months. Hopefully, we will be starting a family to complete everything I ever dreamed of.

It all started so differently though, Simon. When I first saw Graham, it was an instant attraction – me to him. He was tall, very handsome, quite dark-skinned, and one of the most well-dressed men I had ever seen. His suits were always well cut, his shirt neatly ironed and his shoes were always well shined.

In short, he was the sort of man most girls would give a fortune to be seen with. And I was one of them. The trouble is, when he came to work as the boss of the used-car department of the garage where I worked, there was absolutely no way I was of any interest to him whatsoever.

To put it mildly, I was a bit of a mess at that time. I had broken up with my only boyfriend two years before, and I hadn't gone out with anyone else. I had let myself go to pot a little. When I had broken up with Jeff, I had taken refuge in eating. I would eat anything and everything I could get my hands on to cheer myself up.

They weren't big meals, just snacks. But I would have lots and lots of them. Bars of chocolate, bags of crisps, sandwiches – you name it, I would eat it.

I paid absolutely no interest to my clothes, and I never went anywhere, apart from the local wine bar. It was a fairly ordinary existence, but I honestly had no encouragement to break out of it.

I had always been reasonably intelligent, doing well at school, but even though people had said how pretty I had been, it is very hard to feel pretty when you have ballooned up to thirteen and a half stones, and have trouble squeezing into a size sixteen.

Graham was completely out of range, as far as any sort of relationship was concerned. I told my only true friend, Karen – the only person I could really confide in – what a fantastic guy had started to work at the garage.

She told me that if I thought he was that fantastic, why didn't I try to make some sort of contact with him? I told her not to be stupid – why would he be interested in someone like me? Karen asked me if he had a regular girlfriend. As far as I knew he hadn't, but I couldn't see why he would be on the shelf.

But, she did plant the seed of an idea in my mind. Over the course of the next few weeks, work brought Graham and I into a reasonable amount of contact. We got on well. He had a sense of humour that I enjoyed, and I think he knew I wasn't an idiot.

On several occasions, we had to organize promotions – like cheese and wine parties – for the garage, and had to stay behind when it was all over. I found out that he was single, and, although he dated a few girls, there was no one serious in his life.

The night I found all this out, I made a decision that was going to change my life. I never really believed that people's appearances were more important than their characters, but if ever I were going to appeal to a man like Graham, then I would have to put some pride back into my life.

From that point on, I became a different person. I can honestly say that from that moment on, I never touched another bar of chocolate, or a sandwich outside meal times.

I began swimming virtually every day. The first few weeks were really painful. I felt like a whale squeezing into a swimsuit at the local baths. But I did it. When I came out of the changing rooms I sometimes felt that the whole place was staring at me, especially the little children.

I managed to get through a few lengths for the first visits, but slowly and surely, my fitness and my strength built up and I was doing more and more distance. It exhausted me to start with but, gradually, I could cope more and more comfortably.

At the time, I put myself on a diet. I cut out all the junk food I had been eating, and I stuck to salads and vegetables.

You know, the hardest part about trying to change yourself is finding a motive, and, to be honest, Graham was my motive. At first I lived in fear that I would turn up at work and find out he had got married, or engaged. But, after a while, that didn't become the thing that was driving me. I got on the scales at home, and would see the needle moving slowly down. All of a sudden, that became my aim.

I couldn't believe the change coming over me. I started to take an interest in my clothes again. I didn't earn a lot of money, so I picked things that were really smart. And, as my sizes went down – a twelve at first – I felt better and better about myself.

I can't begin to tell you how happy I was the night I went to the baths and plucked up the courage to wear a bikini for the first time. I thought everyone would still point and laugh, but nobody did.

At work, I had energy. I felt confident and happy, and a whole change was coming over me. I went away on holiday for two weeks to Tenerife. When I got back, everyone said how well I looked. Perhaps it was the fact that I had been away – and people saw me in a new light – but everyone seemed to be paying me compliments.

But, of course, there was one I really wanted. And that wasn't long coming. Graham came over to me as soon as I walked through the door of the showroom, and paid me the greatest compliment!

Well, Simon, it didn't take long for that compliment to be an invitation to dinner. And then it didn't take long until we were going out together virtually every night of the week.

As I said, I know physical attraction isn't everything. But if you don't have pride and confidence in yourself, how can you expect other people to have any either?

I put all that back in myself, hoping to win over one man. It worked for me, and I can't begin to tell you how much inspiration it has given me. Please play 'St Elmo's Fire' for me. It is a song that I used to listen to all the way to the swimming baths and back. It really used to drive me on, and it still means an awful lot to me today.

CHAPTER NINE

Battling On

Gill

'Sometimes, there is little you can do to offer help to
someone. Gill, from the South West, claims she is not
brave in how she has coped with life. All I can do is
tell her that she is.'

[BROADCAST: FEBRUARY 1989]

> Don't turn around
> I don't want you seeing me crying
> Just walk away
> 'DON'T TURN AROUND'–ASWAD

I have tried several times to write this; then I think it
isn't really special or good enough for 'Our Tune'. It's
a long story, which has no end, only a beginning. I'm
not strong or special, just a lonely lady trying to pick
up the pieces, find a little bit of happiness, and start all
over again.

It started back in 1974, when I was living in Austr-
alia. My parents had gone there to live. I met and
married a Merchant Naval officer. We came back to
England and settled in the South West.

It wasn't a good marriage and, looking back, I was
never really happy. By 1978, I had had enough and
decided to leave. That was until I got a phone call to
say my mum had had a stroke. I was supposed to
fly to Sydney, but needed to get the money from my
husband.

162

But I was in such a state, I just let him take over. Anyway, I never did get to Sydney, and my mum died. My husband promised to change – he had a bad drinking problem which he took out on me. He did change – I stayed, got pregnant and, for a while, things were a lot better.

When I had my baby, I had a horrific birth. We both 'died' during childbirth, but they managed to save us. Thomas was only five pounds and eleven ounces, but because he was a breech baby, he had a lovely face. It was absolute love at first sight. Maybe because of the complications of the birth or whatever, I loved him so much. He became my whole life.

Unfortunately, the marriage was dreadful. We moved to London, but eventually my husband's treatment of me was so bad, that I became ill. In 1983, I threw him out and got divorced.

I knew it would be hard, and I also knew I would never marry again. I accepted the fact that it would just be me and Thomas. But that didn't matter. We loved each other, and I didn't need anyone else. Being a mother would be enough for me.

My husband had married again, and I was getting a lot of financial aggravation from him. Then, one morning, my son knocked a kettle of boiling water over himself. How I got through that morning, I will never know. I rang an ambulance, keeping him wrapped in wet towels. He lived and has no scars. I was told I was so quick, that I saved his life. All I felt was sick, and so lonely. I'm not a brave lady, and I will never forget being in that hospital all alone. I felt so small and lost.

Life wasn't fun anymore. I don't know why I did what I did next, but it seemed like a good idea at the time. It was the beginning of the end. I sold everything, grabbed my son, and moved back down to the South West.

Maybe I thought that somehow, I would be safer there. I know it's silly, but I loved him so much and I wanted to protect him. We bought this flat, but slowly things got worse. My son began lying and throwing terrible tantrums. If we went out, it would turn into a nightmare. Life was becoming such hell. He was treating me just like his father used to.

I became and still am very depressed. I tried everything, and in the end sought professional help. I guess in my heart I knew what was wrong. He loved, and yet he hated me. The divorce was, to him, my fault.

Anyway, you can imagine how I felt when he suddenly told me that he wanted to go and live with his dad and stepmum. That was in April. Simon, I had to let him go. You see I love him too much to hold on. I couldn't bear to see him unhappy. I have only seen him twice since then, and I don't really know when I will see him again.

He now lives in the Cotswolds, and is very settled and happy. His mummy – she's mummy to him now – has just had a baby, so he has everything he needs. Maybe in time, it will hurt less, but I will never understand why he wanted to go. My song, 'Don't Turn Around', says just how I feel.

For him, I have to keep going. But believe me, I don't want to. I am dreading things like Christmas, as I will be all on my own. I try as hard as I can not to get upset. I know I am not alone and there are a lot of people worse off than me.

But grief is such a personal thing, and it seems as though no one can help. I have now joined my local job club, and go every morning to try to get a job. It is hard to start again when you have lost the only thing in the world you love.

Time will lessen the pain. I am so proud of my little boy; he is only eight years old, but so lovely. I feel so bad writing, as most of the stories are about people who are so brave. But I will keep going. The rest is up to whatever the future holds.

Kate

'*Not every story has a happy ending. And in Kate's case, she is still searching for her happiness.*'
[BROADCAST: FEBRUARY 1989]

> *Don't give up cos you have friends*
> *Don't give up cos you're not beaten yet*
> *Don't give up I know you can make it*
> *good*
> 'DON'T GIVE UP'–PETER GABRIEL AND
> KATE BUSH

I was a rebel during my teens, but my parents coped very well. Then I met Trevor, ten years older than me, but very handsome and attentive. I was 'in love', and we ended up living together.

Although we had been toying with the idea of marriage, we decided to split. I went to divide the savings that we had been putting by for our wedding, and found that gone. Trevor had been a compulsive gambler.

That was a lucky escape, except that seven months later my seven pound, fourteen ounce baby boy was born. Having the new baby, I stayed at home with my mum and dad again. I was given freedom to go out at night, and they adored their little grandson.

Then I met Jerry, and after a whirlwind romance, we were married in 1979. Life was great. He worked away, but on shifts, which meant he was home more often than other men. We found a lovely little flat, and were very happy. Then he was made redundant, just as I became pregnant. The pregnancy lasted for eighteen weeks, and I lost the baby because of all the upset. I desperately wanted another straightaway.

Luck was with us, and three months after the miscarriage, I was pregnant again. Jerry was worried it was too soon, and, again, at sixteen weeks, I lost this one.

In between the two pregnancies, we had moved from our lovely flat to a council maisonette in a rather rough area. Jerry, being out of work, began to spend more and more time with his brother, who lived nearby. He was hell to live with – all he did was complain and complain.

This went on until 1982, when we finally had a beautiful little girl and everything began to look good again. Jerry got a job with a local security firm, but the hours were ridiculous. This got too much and he decided to find a job working away.

Money was tight, but once again mum and dad came to the rescue. They fed me and the two children we now had. They bought them shoes and coats. Meanwhile, Jerry was buying toys for *himself*. He built a model railway in the loft, and thought nothing of spending money on his trains.

Baby number three arrived in 1983. By this time, Jerry was working down south, and only came back one weekend a month. The rot set in. He came home, and sat reading railway magazines, demanding to be fed and looked after.

Here I was with three small children and one large one, who I had married! I never went out, and decided to do something about it before I went mad. I began going out at weekends. Jerry objected, and eventually we separated in late 1985.

Along came a well-dressed, clean-cut man, who gave me back my self-confidence. He was fun; he adored the children; he would take them all out, something which Jerry never did. Everything seemed good, and after six months he moved in.

Six months after that, a problem raised its head. After a day in the garden with the children, I began clearing up when I saw something glinting under a big conifer tree. I lifted up the branches to be confronted by twenty empty Scotch bottles. I was devastated. He denied all knowledge of them. I wanted to believe him, but as the weeks went by, I kept finding them – under my bed, in the airing cupboard, on top of the wardrobe.

Again, I confronted him, and with tears in his eyes, he said he would join AA. He went for weeks, and I thought he would be fine. But the dreaded time for anyone connected with an alcoholic is Christmas, and that soon came around.

It was awful. He got very drunk, and then the violence started. I was thrown around like a rag doll – mentally and physically abused. I could not believe the change in him. I tried to reason with him. I threw him out, and he broke the door down.

More than once he refused to move out. This went on for another eight months, until the beginning of June, when I had to have him removed by the police. He has now moved away.

The last chapter of this is the shortest and the most painful. After a three-year courtship, my sister and her fiancé split up. He and I had always got on well, and he often came over for a cuppa and a chat.

But when he and my sister parted, he began calling around every day. The inevitable happened. He told me he loved me, and I knew I felt the same. I knew him fairly well, and I suggested we keep it quiet until my sister, who had regretted splitting up with him, managed to get over him.

Unfortunately, she found out about us and now thinks that things had been going on for longer than they had. She has told me that as far as she is concerned I no longer exist, and she wishes I was dead.

Dennis and I talked everything over, many times. We decided that once the initial shock was over, and we stayed together, people would realize we were serious. Hopefully, we would be accepted.

He went and explained to my sister that he no longer loved her, but her reaction was to phone him at home and at work, and generally put the pressure on. My mum, who was upset by the whole situation, also phoned him.

One Thursday night, he phoned me and said he would not be coming around anymore. He said that my family would speak to me again if he promised not to see me. I was stunned. I honestly thought he would stand by me. I telephoned him the next day, and told him that I understood, that I had loved him, and that I still loved him. He was upset and apologized over and over again.

The following night, very late, he turned up at my door. Tears in his eyes, he said he could not do it. The saga repeated itself. Although we were much more discreet, my sister saw his car parked opposite my house. She visited him, and begged him not to see me again. The relationship I had with my parents is stretched to breaking point, my sister no longer acknowledges me, and last night I arranged a meeting with Dennis, and realized I had lost him too.

But my life will go on. I have my children and I have lovely memories of those few short weeks I had with Dennis. Our parting was sad and tearful. We sat in his car and said our pieces. He told me he loved me, and I said the same.

I still believe we could have been happy, but I want him to know that I bear him no grudges. All I can say is that the song sums it all up: 'Don't Give Up'.

Pete

'*The hardest part about relationships is talking to each other. Many people write to tell me that they think they'd still be with their loved one, if they had talked more. Pete found that out the hard way.*'

[BROADCAST: APRIL 1990]

> *Show me one more sign*
> *Give me one more time*
> *Cos you give me, you give me*
> *temptation baby*
>
> 'TEMPTATION'–WET WET WET

It was two years ago that I first met Sarah, at a friend's sister's wedding. I was nineteen and Sarah was seventeen. My sister, who I had not seen for a while, started doing her matchmaking, and, by the end of the night, Sarah and I were sitting in a corner talking like old friends.

I walked her back to where she was staying that night, and we talked until three-thirty the next morning. With neither of us having had a serious relationship before, I was more than a bit apprehensive about asking her to the pictures that Sunday. But she accepted, and that was the start of our seeing each other.

Sarah was perfect. She got on well with my family and friends, and after a while I met her family. As I was seeing Sarah all the time, she lost touch with her college friends. We always went out with *my* friends.

Sarah never moaned about what we did at the weekend, but I never asked her what she wanted to do. After the first couple of months, Sarah stopped talking and I stopped listening.

Christmas 1989 came and went, and we were still quite happy. I was playing rugby on Saturdays, with training Mondays and Thursdays, football on Sundays, with football training on Wednesdays. I was thinking of myself more and more.

Sarah was trying to talk to me, and I was always thinking of myself. Sarah was still always there, not saying a bad word to or about me. We went on holiday during the Summer of 1989, and it was after another day of my doing just what I wanted, that Sarah decided she'd had enough. We talked and sorted out our problems, but I didn't learn.

After we came back, things settled down into the old groove – me borrowing money from Sarah to take her out. Once, when we were out with my mates, I started putting her down, and making her so upset. After getting all I ever wanted, I was taking it all for granted. My family were all asking me why I treated her so badly. But you don't realize until it is too late.

I didn't realize that I was pushing Sarah into a corner, but on 10 February 1989, Sarah decided that enough was enough, and on our way back from a disco, she told me we were finished.

We talked a little that night, and it dawned on me that because she couldn't talk to me, and because she had no girlfriends to talk to, she had been getting close to one of my friends. I questioned her about their relationship, and Sarah admitted that, becasue he was the only person to talk to, they had become more than friends.

I didn't sleep that Saturday night, and when I phoned Sarah on the Sunday, she had already gone out with my friend. I phoned her on Monday, and asked her to let me meet her after work, to talk about our problems.

I told Sarah that I didn't blame her, as I knew it was my fault. I listened to her for the first time in months. That night was the closest that we had ever been. But I have still lost the only person I ever wanted, and it is all my fault. It is only now that I realize how much I really love her.

Ruth

'Some love affairs are so sad, it seems hard to believe that people can cope with their emotions. Ruth – not her real name – told me one of the saddest.'

[BROADCAST: MARCH 1990]

> *If you see me walking down the street*
> *And I start to cry each time we meet*
> *Walk on by*

'WALK ON BY'– DIONNE WARWICK

My heart is breaking while I'm writing this letter. Today, after a lot of soul-searching, and coming to a heart-rending decision, I've said goodbye to the only man I have ever loved and adored. His name is Stuart.

I met him five years ago at a disco. It was love at first sight. We talked and danced together, and found we had a lot in common. At that time he was very mixed-up emotionally, having been divorced for only a couple of months, and then having been made redundant from his job.

I couldn't help admiring him from the start. Through all his troubles, he still managed to joke and laugh at his predicament. I knew it was all a front; I could see right through it. But it was his sense of humour that helped pull him through.

We started going out together, and every moment spent with him was a whole bundle of fun. He got himself together, and started up his own haulage business. He was anxious and dubious about it to start with, but I knew it would succeed. And succeed he did!

Our relationship was good. Not only did we become lovers, but we became the best of friends. We were able to talk openly to each other about everything and anything. Stuart's only problem was being unable to make a commitment.

I guess his messy divorce prevented him being able to do so. I never pressured him, as much as I loved and wanted him. Looking back, maybe this was my downfall, because I knew he really did care for me. I guess maybe I stood too far back, and by doing that, someone else came on the scene. We never had any secrets from each other. Being the good friends we were, Stuart was able to tell me about her.

We parted as friends, but in a funny sort of way, still needed each other. Stuart would phone me up, and come round and see me, even though he was going out with her. I was always there for him. I loved him so much, and I would just melt into his arms when he came around. This part of our relationship was so special and wonderful. I always had the hope that one day he would realize we were meant for each other.

My hopes were dashed when Stuart called round last year to tell me she was pregnant! I was devastated.

Knowing Stuart as well as I do, I knew he would stand by her. He did, but he still called round to see me. Each time, I just melted into his arms. He said he would never get married, but would stand by her for the baby's sake.

The baby was born in October – a baby girl. I didn't see Stuart for a while. In December, just before Christmas, he called round again. He was chuffed to bits with his little girl, but still maintained he wouldn't get married. I guess at the back of my mind there was still a glimmer of hope for me. I loved him so much. In January he called around again. Once again, I found myself with him. I'm like a magnet to him.

This time he told me that she and the baby had moved in with him. He left me that day, and I didn't see him again until today. I knew he would call round again soon. In that short space of time, I came to my heart-breaking decision to break off contact with him completely.

These last few weeks have been a nightmare for me. My head was telling me one thing, and my heart was telling me another. I don't want to be the thorn in the side of that beautiful baby's life. I know that if the boot were on the other foot, and I was the one in her position, I would be feeling very worried and insecure. I know my decision to end it all, is the right one for everybody concerned.

It has broken my heart to do it. I'll never love anyone as much as I love Stuart. I love him enough to let him go. My only hope is that he will be very happy. I wish him all the love, luck and happiness in the world, and if she loves him as much as I do, then he is one hell of a lucky guy.

I won't ever forget him. He will always remain in my heart, and, who knows, maybe one day I'll find somebody. I'd like to think that in time I will. Until then, if Stuart is happy, then my sacrifice will have been worth it.

Stuart knows the sort of person I am, and has respected my decision after I told him. He held me for the last time today. Now I feel terrible. I know when the tears stop falling, and the pain eases, I'll get on with my life without him.

Stuart knows I've written. I told him I would. He is a deeply sensitive person with a heart of gold. There is a song which is so relevant today – 'Walk on by', by Dionne Warwick.

Kerry

'*When you get a letter like this one from Kerry – she asked me to change her name – there's no need to say anything. She sums up her own emotions brilliantly.*'
[BROADCAST: NOVEMBER 1989]

> *Can you hear me this time*
> *I see the storm grow*
> *There's a light in the desert tonight*
> 'TENDER HANDS'–CHRIS DE BURGH

I'm afraid it's another sad 'Our Tune'. But, perhaps, sharing it will help myself and other people. I met Patrick when, at eighteen, I left London and went up to college. I was still a virgin, full of hope and aspirations, and all the usual youthful desires – half-consciously looking for someone to fall in love with.

Pretty soon it happened, though I didn't realize it at first. We had rooms near each other at the university residences. First, it was a matter of just smiling at each other in corridors, and before and after lectures. Then, after a while, everything happened suddenly. We ran into each other at the student union bar, had a few drinks too many and went back to his room.

I still remember waking up to the most beautiful moment in my life. The birds were singing outside, the sun filtered through the curtains, and, next to me, lay Patrick.

Later that day, I rushed down to the doctor to sort out contraception, and our love continued. Once, I remember, we made love on a deserted beach. But that turned out to be the last day of our affair.

It came out that I was pregnant from that first, heavenly night. When I told Patrick this, he looked at me blankly and said to me, 'Well, that's your problem.' I think he was simply scared.

Because I wanted my degree and the prospect of a career, I decided to have the pregnancy terminated, somewhat against my conscience. I wanted to discuss it with Patrick, but he avoided me, even moving out of his rooms so that I couldn't find him.

I felt so foolish going into hospital, another stupid teenager getting into trouble. Before, I'd have looked down on anyone careless enough to get into such a position, but now I'm deeply sympathetic of anyone who finds themselves in that position.

I took time off my course, and came back to live with my parents in London. They were very sympathetic. Some time after, I received a letter from a friend. It told me that Patrick had died in a road accident. He was twenty years old.

It was only then that I realized how much I still loved him, and how it wasn't his fault that he couldn't cope with the pregnancy. But the most awful thing was that I had killed the child, in whom he could have lived on.

When I went back to Leicester, where I was at college, every minute was an agony – every street reminded me of him, how we'd walked and kissed there. I took the next train back. The memories were too much. I'll never be able to face the place again.

In the first days of our relationship, he would play a record that seemed to sum up our relationship then, and my emotions now – 'Tender Hands', by Chris de Burgh

Patrick, it turns me upside down each time I think of you.

Jenny

'One of the greatest tragedies is the damage caused to people's lives by drunk drivers. Jenny's story shows how.'

[BROADCAST: JANUARY 1987]

> *I want your love action*
> *Love's just a distraction*
> *No talking, just looking*
> 'LOVE ACTION'–HUMAN LEAGUE

After all I've been through with my boyfriend this year, I felt I ought to tell you my story as a warning to others, and to make drunk drivers realize what they make other people go through.

Jack and I met at a guide/scout camp about four and a half years ago, when we were both thirteen. He was the one who had crept into my tent and started to chat me up. I was, and still am, very quiet and shy, although

I was very flattered by all the attention he was giving me. On the last day, he asked me if I would be his girlfriend. I said yes, not knowing how serious our relationship would be.

After this, there followed three years of typical teen-age romance – arguments, other girls or boys, and all the normal things. On my sixteenth birthday, Jack bought me an engagement ring.

However, we knew no one would take it seriously, so we kept it to ourselves. In February of 1987, we had our biggest argument over another girl, who I found he had been seeing as well as me.

I threw my ring back at him, and walked out on him. But after about two months, we saw each other again on a bus, while I was with my new boyfriend. Jack wrote to me, asking me if I would go back out with him again.

From then on, it became much more of a serious relationship. Everything went fine, until the summer, when Jack was given the sack from his job. As usual, he came out fine, as he had been offered another job within two weeks.

In September, he joined the Territorial Army, and had to go away for a fortnight. On the morning that he left me, I found out that I was pregnant. I couldn't tell my parents, and I couldn't tell any friends.

Keeping it to myself was nearly impossible. I told one friend but it all came out, and everyone knew. I wanted to kill myself to end it all. When Jack came back, we decided that it would be best to end the pregnancy.

In October, we saved enough money and travelled down to London to end the pregnancy. The place was awful, packed with people with the same problem. After I came out, I felt so much better. We were going to start another life, as if none of it had happened.

Just when we thought things were going to work out

for us, Jack was driving to join the Territorial Army when he was involved in a head-on collision with a drunk driver. Thankfully, there was a paramedic on the scene, who gave him the fluids he needed. It took firemen over an hour to cut him out of the car. He was rushed to a hospital in Wrexham, where they operated on him for four hours.

On being told that his chances of survival were literally nil, his parents called me. Since then, Jack has defied all the doctors. He is still alive, and should be coming out of intensive care some time next week.

However, the real meaning of this letter is to try to make all those people who even think of drinking and driving not to do it. If they had to go through what Jack has gone through, they would know how he feels.

Even for us – his family and friends – to see Jack lying there with broken ribs, bruised lungs, a broken leg, a broken ankle, compound fractures in his other ankle, a smashed liver, a cut ear, a bruised chest, and other injuries, is awful.

To see him lying there, not being able to communicate, and being frustrated that no one understands him is horrific. At times, he blames us and shouts at us, and no matter how hard we try, we cannot get through to him.

Things cannot get worse for both of us. I'm not even sure he'll come out of this still loving me. No matter what, though, I'll always love him.

Gwyneth

'So many times, I hear from listeners who have fallen for someone, only to discover that they stand no chance of winning their love. Gwyneth's story is typical of that.'

[BROADCAST: JULY 1988]

> Weren't you the one who tried to hurt
>   me with goodbye
> Did I crumble, did you think I'd lay
>   down and die
> Oh no not I, I will survive
>   'I WILL SURVIVE'–GLORIA GAYNOR

I have changed the names in my letter for obvious reasons, but I hope it might make other people stop and think about doing the same sort of thing.

It all started when I began working a couple of nights a week behind the bar in a nice little pub. I had only been there for a month when Nick walked in. I can say that we looked at each other, and just clicked. There was this nice feeling of instant mutual attraction.

But nothing happened and nothing was said. He didn't come in again until a few nights later, and still only the eye contact happened, with me being quite shy. I thought maybe he was too.

I happened to be in the pub socially one night, when he came in. It was really strange. He didn't attempt any of the usual chat-up. We just talked naturally, as if we'd known each other for ages.

I told him when I worked, and the next night he came in and that's when he told me of his feelings for me. He said he thought it was love at first sight, that he didn't know why it had happened, but that it just had. But he also told me that he was married. I know I should have left it there and then, but I just couldn't. He told me he had two little boys, of whom he thought the world. He said he cared for his wife, and even loved her in his own way, but that his marriage was built on friendship.

I thought that was fair enough. At least he hadn't denied that he cared for her a great deal, and, despite his situation, he was, and still is, a very nice, caring person. Anyway, the relationship got deeper and deeper, and we both got more and more emotionally involved. We would phone each other every day, and see each other whenever we could. Then reality had to stick its big ugly nose in, because at the end of July, I discovered I was seven weeks pregnant.

At the time I found out, I just cried and cried my heart out, because even though I knew what had to be done, the thought that I had something inside me from both of us gave me a wonderful feeling.

But it wasn't to be. You see, I already have a five-year-old son, who I love dearly, from another relationship which didn't work out. We lived with my mother, who is such a lovely person. It would have broken her heart to have found out about Nick.

So a friend of mine made arrangements for me to go to the British Pregnancy Advice Bureau. Nick and I went, and the termination was arranged for the next week. It was a real eye-opening experience. I will never forget the feelings. Most of it all passed by in a daze, as if it weren't really happening to me. Then, to top it all, about a month later, Nick's wife found out about him and me.

After that, my world just fell apart, because I realized that Nick could never leave his wife and children, and he had his own business to think of. He said his wife depended on him – he was her security.

I was destroyed. I felt rejected, and thought about all the mental pain I went through with the termination. I had done all this for other people, one of them him, even though he said he would have stood by me whatever choice I made.

After that, I fell into a deep depression. I couldn't eat or sleep. I didn't bother to get dressed half the time; I just wanted the days to pass quickly. I wanted to wake up and feel all right. I couldn't even find the energy to pick up my son from school.

I just didn't realize that my being unhappy was making him unhappy. Nick was still around through all this, phoning me to see if I was OK, and seeing me whenever he could get out of the house.

I suffered panic attacks because of the depression. I tried tranquillizers, group therapy and even a psychiatrist, who told me I was strong minded, and could make it back on my own. So I started the long haul back from the floor.

Nick was still there, phoning me every day. In his own way, I think he still loved me. In October, my son and I moved to our own little house, and I knew then that I had to get things together for his sake. Two weeks before Christmas, I ended my relationship with Nick. He tried to talk me out of it. He thought I needed and depended on him.

But I realized that all I was doing was waiting for the time he could sneak a few hours here and there to get out and see me. I wanted more than that. I wanted a secure relationship, so I ended it.

I still think about him every day. Because of the termination, I developed a problem, which means it'll be unlikely I'll ever be able to have children again. I think I've been paid back enough.

Nick still phones from time to time, but I'll get through it. I've learned a very painful lesson, but now I'm almost myself again. I have chosen the song 'I Will Survive', because I honestly think I will.

Tom

'It is hard to see how much you love someone until they're not there. Tom's story shows just how difficult it is.'

[BROADCAST: FEBRUARY 1987]

> *It'll get you in the end*
> *It's God's revenge, know it's wrong*
> *Tell me why is it I'm diggin' your scene*
> 'DIGGIN' YOUR SCENE'–THE BLOW MONKEYS

I first met Alison, who was to become my wife, back in March 1985, and at first everything was absolutely great between us. I mean, we had a couple of fallings out, like most young couples do, but we always made it up.

Then, two years later, I joined the Territorial Army. This meant I had to be away a lot, and eventually the times I spent with the TA began to cause more rows. Alison and I split. I was desperately upset about it, but I tried to forget all about it by going away with the TA as much as I could.

One Saturday night, we had a massive campfire. All the soldiers were around it, singing and having a great time. There were female soldiers on the exercises with us, so we all started talking. I spotted a young lady on her own, so I went over and we began talking.

We got on really well. She told me her name was Robin, and we just had a great deal of fun. The night went by so quickly. When it was all over, we swapped our addresses and phone numbers. A week went by, and she didn't phone. I eventually plucked up the courage to phone her, and made arrangements for us to meet.

We spent a great day, walking around, and getting to know each other a bit better. I made plans for Robin and I to spend one day a week together. But, each time I was with Robin, I couldn't stop thinking about Alison.

I'd be wondering what she was doing, or who she was with. Even though the relationship with Robin got stronger and stronger, I couldn't get Alison out of my mind.

A few days later, I found out that Alison was going out with different fellows. That really hurt me badly. It got so bad that I couldn't think of anything else. And it really started to affect things with Robin. She couldn't take the terrible mood swings and the depressions I was going through. We had a massive row, and parted.

Once she was out of my life as well, I just broke down. I sent a letter to her, and got no reply for months and months. Finally, she wrote and told me she had bought a house in Edinburgh. I've sent her another letter asking if she'll spend a holiday with me.

It's now all too late for Alison. We have no chance of going back together, and we have filed for divorce. So now I'm just picking up the pieces and trying to get my life back together.

All I can say to other people is that if a relationship

breaks down, you must, above anything else, try to keep your head up and keep going.

Carol

'Sticking together through thick and thin. That's what's love is all about. Carol's story shows you just how.'
[BROADCAST: JANUARY 1987]

> *Now you've got the best of me*
> *Come on and take the rest of me*
> *You to me are everything*
> 'YOU TO ME ARE EVERYTHING'
> –THE REAL THING

I was brought up in a small village in Scotland. The eldest child of our family was an alcoholic, my mum was widowed, and I was picked on at school for being ugly. I was so often ridiculed that I just buried myself in my studies and my family.

When I was fifteen, my mum remarried and had a child. I felt I was being given up for the new man and child in her life. At seventeen, I left home to go to college in Edinburgh. I found it difficult to make friends, and felt desperate to prove myself by finding a man. I felt so inadequate and ugly. I always seemed to be the one who walked home alone.

Then I found the kind of man who was interested in me – the married type who didn't care what I looked like just as long as I was there for him.

I lost my virginity to him at seventeen, and then went

on to have relationships with a man who was going out with someone else, and another one who was married.

I was sexually attacked by a man I thought was my friend, and on top of that, failed miserably at college. I decided that the time had come to run away and try to start a new life for myself. I came down to London to work as a nanny. The parents I was working for were really horrible to their kids. They beat and starved them, so I mentioned it to a social worker, and the kids were taken to hospital.

A court case followed, which was very ugly. I was accused of being interfering, self-centred, and, after the parents were given a suspended sentence, I felt guilty that I had ruined four people's lives.

My new start in London wasn't going too well. I felt things would improve if I could meet some new people, so I joined a dating agency. I met a couple of other people, who seemed to confirm everything bad I had ever heard about dating agencies! I was seriously considering another new start.

But one guy rang up. A musician, called Roy. He was twenty, but to be honest, I was so fed up by the whole thing, I tried to put him off. But he rang back, and we met. We got on really well together, and after a few months, I decided to move into the flat he shared with his friend.

It was hellish! I think that after years of feeling like I was the most worthless person on earth, I had to put Roy to every possible task to make him prove that he really did like me, and wasn't just using me like everyone else.

Roy was in a band at the time, and they had a female drummer. Roy used to have to go to rehearsals at the studios under her flat. When I met her, she told me she was surprised that Roy had a girlfriend, because whenever he had been at the studios, he made advances at her!

The relationship was near breaking point, and I went back to Scotland for a holiday. I realized for the first time that, after a year with Roy, I had fallen head over heels in love. That wasn't what I expected – I thought it would have been sudden, loud, and mind-blowing. But it had happened quietly, slowly and surely. I couldn't wait to get back to tell him.

We've been together for two years now, and I still find it hard to believe that he stuck with it when I was taking out on him all the mistrust I had built up over the years. He's helped me to believe in myself, and I've become the sort of person I always wanted to be – but never thought I could.

We're getting married, and that's just the beginning. I've made a promise to myself to repay his trust by making each day better than the day before.

Patricia

'Patricia discovered you cannot play with other people's emotions, without problems.'
[BROADCAST: SEPTEMBER 1989]

> *What have I got to do to be heard*
> *What do I say when it's all over*
> *And sorry seems to be the hardest word*
> 'SORRY SEEMS TO BE THE HARDEST
> WORD'–ELTON JOHN

This starts right back in 1984. I went for a weekend

with friends down to Brighton for a crazy time. Our car kept breaking down, and every time it broke down, four guys would appear to help us with it. One guy was Graham. I knew immediately that I had fallen head over heels. They say you can fall head over heels – or in love at first sight. Well, I did. Graham was in the Army, and we started seeing each other; obviously, it was very difficult. Graham went to Ireland and we lost touch. I never forgot him; I wanted to write but didn't know where.

I started going out with friends again after a period of about three months. In 1986, I met Colin, and while I was going with him, I was thinking of Graham. I kept telling myself that it was no use, and that I had to get on with my life. Looking back, I was being very cruel to Colin. I loved him, but not totally; there was something missing. Anyway, I fell pregnant and Colin and I decided to get married – with the pressure from both families we thought it was the best thing to do.

Just after we were married in October 1986, Graham wrote to me and told me he loved me and wanted to be with me. I had to tell him that I was married and expecting a baby in January. Of course, Graham rang me and explained that all that didn't matter to him. We talked about all the good times we had had and, of course, it all came flooding back – the memories and the feeling of one hundred per cent love. We started to write regularly, and the feelings grew stronger.

In January 1987 I gave birth to a lovely little girl. Colin was over the moon, and I was the happiest woman in the world. To have this lovely tiny human all my own – the only thing missing was Graham.

After the birth of Carey, I started getting snappy with Colin, and things started getting really bad. It all came to a head when Graham came to see me. Colin was still at home. I had to make a decision – Colin or Graham.

After a lot of heartache and thought I chose to stay with Colin for Carey's sake – I would just have to get on as best as I could.

Graham could not take this, and joined the Foreign Legion. Things got worse between Colin and me. Obviously, Colin felt he could not trust me, and started telling me I could not go out. In fact, I was allowed out once a week with my best friend Jo, other than that, I had to stay at home. Colin started going out drinking and coming home angry – say no more! Needless to say Colin and I split up in May of last year.

Graham has been in touch, but things will not be the same. I still love him very much and think about him all the time. I have spent the last year feeling very guilty. Not only have I ruined Colin's life, but I have upset the balance of my daughter's life and I have let down all the people that have loved and trusted me. I just wish I could make it up, but, of course, it is too late.

I just want to say sorry for all the hurt I have caused Colin and the families – and especially Carey. If you choose this letter, I would like as my tune: 'Sorry Seems to be the Hardest Word', by Elton John.

Annette

'*Annette, from Manchester, gave her man more than enough chances to bring her happiness. He didn't and in the end she had to look after herself.*'
[BROADCAST: JANUARY 1989]

> *I'll be there for you if you should need*
>   *me*
> *You don't have to change a thing*
> *I love you just the way you are*
> 'NOTHING'S GONNA CHANGE MY LOVE FOR YOU'
> –GLEN MADEIROS

The only way I can start my story, Simon, is by saying that I have met the most fantastic man anyone could wish to meet. We started seeing each other regularly a couple of times a week.

Then, as time went on, David wanted to see me more and more. But there was a problem, something I hadn't told him. I had a little boy, Drew, who was sixteen months old.

We went out for the day, while my mum looked after Drew, and I told him all about my son. He was upset that I had not trusted him enough to be able to tell when we started going out together.

I told him the real reason I hadn't told him was that I didn't want to lose his friendship. It was important to me, because he had been the only man I had dated since I had ended with Drew's father.

After that, he wanted to know why I had broken up with Drew's father. I told him that he'd beaten me numerous times, and when I had had Drew, he had beaten up both of us. Drew was only eight weeks old when he ended up in hospital because of the injuries his father had caused him. After that, we parted, and he hadn't seen Drew since.

Well, when Drew's father found out I was seeing another man, he started court proceedings to get access to Drew. Since May last year, I have been backwards and forwards to court. David, thankfully, has stood by me all this time, and Drew and I have moved in to live with him. In July last year, Drew started calling David 'Daddy', and life could not have been more perfect.

All the time, I was going to court, really believing that they wouldn't be able to grant an animal like my ex any access to my son. After a fantastic family Christmas, when everything seemed perfect with Drew and David, I suddenly received a court order, in which they granted my ex access to his son every other weekend.

I am petrified that David wil not be able to stand this. He has started to think of Drew as his, and I honestly believe that it will confuse my son, not knowing who he should be calling his Daddy.

I am not sure what will happen. I know that Drew's father will probably only keep up his rights to visit Drew for a few weeks, as he has to travel a long way, and he doesn't really have any great interest in the boy.

But I'm scared that this pressure will be too much for David to cope with, on top of all we've gone through. If it does scare David off, all I can sincerely hope for is that he finds someone to love and care for him as much as I do, and to let him know that if he needs someone, I will always be here for him.

It seems so terribly wrong. David has changed my life so much. He is a complete gentleman – so kind and considerate. And a real no-gooder, who beats his woman and his eight-week-old child, can shatter all the happiness.

I wish he would just leave me alone. He had plenty of chances with me when we were together, but now, he simply wants to ruin my life and my chance to start again. But I have to let David know that I will always love him, and that I hope we can get through all this together.

Lorraine

'*Lorraine found life got on top of her completely, and drove her to despair. But she wrote to me from Kent to tell me how everything has worked out.*'

[BROADCAST: SEPTEMBER 1987]

> *Never gonna give you up*
> *Never gonna let you down*
> *Never gonna run around and desert*
>   *you*
> 'NEVER GOING TO GIVE YOU UP'–RICK ASTLEY

I'm no great-looker, Simon. In fact, I'm a very, very plain Jane. But I have found the most wonderful, kindest human being in the world – and all I want to do is tell him how much I love him.

I never thought I would ever be the sort of person to attract a tall, dark handsome man, who any woman would love. But I have, and I want to tell you my story.

My life had been sort of normal. I was adopted as a child, but I loved my stepparents dearly, and still do. Even though I got four out of five O-levels at school, I had no idea how I did it, because I became a bit of a rebel.

Anyway, after school I went to live with a very good friend of mine called Sybill. I lived with her until I joined the WRAF at the age of seventeen. It was the best thing I did in years, helping me to develop a streak of responsibility, independence and some leadership qualities. Anyway, that's where I met Simon.

Two years later, we got married. I was nineteen, and honestly thought I loved him. But the day after the wedding, I knew it was a mistake. But I was young enough, and thought that perhaps love would grow. After a year, we had a little boy, Richard, and everything was fine. I was fond of Simon, but still didn't love him as such. Three years later, we had a little girl, Penny. We were a 'family', but nothing ever seemed to go right for us.

This was one thing that annoyed me. I told him we would go and see his mother about fifteen to sixteen times a year, and every Christmas, but to get him to go and see my parents was like getting blood out of a stone.

In the eleven years we were married, we saw my family only six times. When we did visit them, it was only for a few hours. He even got me believing that my family didn't want anything to do with me, and hated me. But I later found out that it was Simon they couldn't stand the sight of, but they were too kind to say anything.

Nine years after Penny was born, I became pregnant again, even though I was on the Pill at the time. The baby was born, and things went on much as they had before. Well, along with doubts, bills were mounting up, many of which he had collected, so I went to work at a nearby RAF camp. It was only part-time evening work, but it started to help us pay everything off.

I enjoyed work, even to the point of going in an hour early – anything to get away from his moaning and complaining. I took everything from him, abuse, threats, insults, just because *he* couldn't face up to his financial responsibilities.

After eleven years, without telling him, I filed for divorce. But then, he started complaining again about how he didn't have any money in his pocket – if he had less than £20 in his pocket he'd be complaining he was broke, and expected me to help him out all the time.

I turned and told him that I had filed for divorce. He got up and smashed my smoked-glass wall unit with his fist. He ended up at hospital to have stitches put into it. When he came home, he pointed to the unit and said, 'Doesn't that prove to you that I love you?'

I told him that it only showed me he was stupid enough to stick his fist through a piece of glass, and I went off to work. At work, I had a few good friends I could talk to, without them telling everyone what I had told them. There was Laura, who had been through what I had been going through, and there was Norman.

He was a great listener. They both helped me so much. The divorce went through. My friends came around to see me, to make sure I was all right.

Norman, especially, was very good to me. We would have some laughs, we would talk, and we found out that we had a tremendous amount in common. What started as friendship, slowly became something else. Well, the inevitable happened, and we ended up in bed together. Even though I was still on the Pill, three months later I found out I was expecting.

I wasn't sure how Norman would take it. I thought: There goes a great relationship, before it's really even had a chance to get started. I told him the news after a while. He paused for a while, then said, 'If *you* think you can cope with another child, then *we'll* have it.'

Norman added that he would also wait until I was ready for a new commitment, then we could marry and legally become man and wife.

Now, we have little Julie to complete our family. All the other children are calling him Daddy, and, after we all sat down together around the table, we decided to live together as a family.

I sometimes get very depressed, and feel that all the things I have been through are still haunting me. But Norman is always there to give me a cuddle and a kiss. Everyone thinks of us as a family – which we are, with our normal ups and downs. But at least he deals with the house, unlike my ex-husband.

He has even said that he will become a house-husband for me, if I want to go back to work. He is the kindest man I have ever met, and I'll never get over just how lucky I am to have salvaged something from my life.

CHAPTER TEN

Love Against the Odds

Leah

'When I read this letter – Leah is not her real name –
I was so touched at the way it showed how real love
will always survive the toughest test.'

[BROADCAST: JANUARY 1989]

> You're once, twice
> Three times a lady
> And I love you
> 'THREE TIMES A LADY'–THE COMMODORES

It all began in July 1983. I had not been back long from
travelling overland to Kathmandu. I was nineteen. My
sister dragged me out to a dinner party organized by
the karate club she went to. I played gooseberry all
evening, not knowing anyone – until she pointed out
her instructor, Tim. I'll always remember her comment:
'You'd match each other' because of the colour of the
clothes we were wearing.

There was an instant attraction – not quite love at
first sight, perhaps, but something sparked off between
us. We danced, we talked, we had that special last slow
dance together. It was like we'd known each other for
a long time.

We went out every night for the next week. Mum
was slightly apprehensive at first – when she found out
that he was twelve years older than me. The first night

that Tim and I didn't see each other was one Friday night.

As I was getting ready to go out with my sister, I collapsed and had an epileptic fit. No warning – I hadn't even fainted in my life. My parents were obviously worried. I couldn't tell Tim because he was in a small flat by himself, with no phone.

I was scared enough, and I was worried he'd be scared off. He was exactly the opposite. Sometimes when we were alone together, when I had a *petit-mal* attack, he'd comfort me and help me to relax. It was three months of that before I could be given medication – I had to wait for a brain scan in Brighton.

And, all that summer, I told Tim not to fall in love with me, because I was off to college that September, miles away in Manchester. But we knew it was too late. By the time I left, we were crazy about each other. We wrote; we phoned. It was agony, missing him for three whole years, only broken up with wonderful romantic holidays.

We got engaged on 22 December 1984 – although he had actually proposed to me in September of the year before. I finished college in June 1986 – at last we were together! I would have married straightaway, but apart from a lack of money, we realized we hadn't been together for more than three months at any one time.

I moved in with him. We were so happy. But the rot seemed to set in when I asked to start making arrangements for the wedding. We were living in a tiny, depressing, one-room bedsit, designed for one. I decided this wasn't the life for me, and one awful January night, I walked out. My friends couldn't believe it – they asked why. And, really, I didn't have an answer. I didn't know why.

We went out for a special meal on his birthday in February. We realized how much we meant to each other. Within two months, we moved to a four-room flat away from town. And we decided that if we were going to be back together, we'd have to make a real commitment. We did.

We finally named the date. And when we married, it was exactly six years and six days after we first met. 'Our Tune' is the one we always listened to when we were apart, 'Three Times a Lady', by the Commodores.

The one message I have is that, despite the hurdles of being apart and coming to terms with something like epilepsy, we made it through the hard times. An age difference of twelve years doesn't matter one little bit – we love each other, and that's all that matters.

Maeve

'Maeve's letter shows just how strong love can be. And it shows just what can happen if you can find a little compassion in your heart as well'.
[BROADCAST: DECEMBER 1988]

> *I want to know what love is*
> *I want you to show me*
> *I want to feel what love is*
> 'I WANT TO KNOW WHAT LOVE IS'
> –FOREIGNER

This all began two years ago, when I came home from work, thinking I was going out for the night with my husband. I bought myself a new dress, had a bath, got dressed and thought to myself how nice I looked.

An hour went by, then another. I thought: He's forgotten all about it – he's probably drinking somewhere, as he often does. As I went upstairs, I went past his wardrobe, which was open. To my horror, all his clothes had gone. Panic struck me. What was happening? I rushed downstairs, looking for some kind of letter explaining what was going on.

I finally came across it. It was a 'Dear John' letter, saying he had left for another woman with three children, saying how much he wanted a family, that he was sorry for doing it to me this way. He told me I should find someone else. How could I? I didn't want anyone else. It was him I loved and wanted. I had been married to him for fourteen years, and was unable to have any children.

I'd had many operations in the hope of getting pregnant, but it never worked. Now he'd gone. I broke down and cried, sobbing, and wondering how he could do it.

People might say that I should have known that something was going on, but everything was all right between us. We didn't argue any more than usual; our sex life was the same. Anyway, I turned to drink. As soon as the pubs opened, I would be there. I would stay there until closing, anything to take my mind off him. I just couldn't forget him after fourteen years.

He was all I had got. I was lost without him. My life was now so empty. It was then I decided to take my own life. I shut all the curtains so I wouldn't be disturbed. I was crying; I couldn't stop. It was like that every morning until every night. Then I paused for thought. I didn't think of my husband – he was in love with this other woman, so he wouldn't have been upset if I took my own life.

I thought of my parents, brothers and sisters. How would they take it? I knew it would affect them very badly. So I suddenly decided not to do it. A year went by. I was having a party at my house, just to cheer myself up a bit, when there was a knock on the door. To my surprise, it was my husband. My heart started to pound away.

I tried to act calm, asking him what he wanted. He said he had heard there was a party at my house, and asked if he could come in. I said yes. We had a dance, and everyone was really happy for me. Then we went outside for a talk. He said he had left the other woman. I asked him why. He said it was because he was still in love with me. He asked if I would take him back.

It didn't take too much thinking over, as I still loved him very much. So I said yes. He hugged me, saying he would never leave me again. I know that people will say I shouldn't have taken him back, but I couldn't bear to lose him again. So I did what my heart told me to do, and that was to have him back.

We didn't sleep together straightaway. That took some time. Anyway, that was two years ago, and things are really happening for us now. At the moment, we are fostering a two-year-old girl. We have had her for five months, and we love her very much. I'm also having treatment at a London hospital for a second attempt at a test-tube baby of our own.

I hope it works this time, as we don't have a lot of money, and couldn't really afford another attempt. But, if we do have a child, then our happiness really will be complete. 'Our Tune' is by Foreigner, and is 'I Want to Know What Love is'. It really reminds me of the time when everything was going wrong, but it also reminds me of how much happiness I have found now.

Fiona

'Fiona's letter was one of the most remarkable. How she managed to turn her life around is a lesson to everyone.'

[BROADCAST: DECEMBER 1988]

> *I love you baby like a flower loves the*
> *spring*
> *And I love you baby like a robin loves*
> *to sing*
> *I love you baby River Deep, Mountain*
> *High*
>
> 'RIVER DEEP, MOUNTAIN HIGH'
> –IKE AND TINA TURNER

I was divorced in 1980, after ten years of a rather stormy marriage. I had four sons, and I was determined that I would never get involved with another man. I dedicated myself to my sons, but like so many single parents, found life very lonely. I was able to cope with day-to-day life, although things were rough financially.

But the worst times were the evenings, when the boys were in bed. And Sundays, they were awful. Everywhere I looked there were couples. I felt so alone. All my friends were married, so if I went out with the girls, the husbands would feel threatened in case I took their wives on a manhunt. There seems to be a terrible stigma about divorced wives. They're supposed to be frustrated nymphomaniacs! They are really only lonely people looking for some company.

My parents were great, giving me loads of support, but I was still a very lonely person. I had to do something, something to give my boys and myself a way out of the black hole we were sinking into.

Through a social worker who had occasional coffee mornings, I met another female single parent who had two children. We realized the lack of facilities for one-parent families, so decided to start a group of Gingerbread in our hometown.

We took a few weeks arranging premises, contacting National Gingerbread for advice, drawing posters, and advertising. In April of 1982, we told the social worker the date and place of our first meeting, and were not really expecting much response.

To our surprise, sixteen turned up, mostly female. I think there were only three men. Things began to look a bit brighter; we had a purpose, a place to go, arrangements to make. We were among people with similar problems, but very different situations. We began to arrange outings, picnics – helping each other with transport and home repairs. We also knew there was always a shoulder to cry on when needed. The children made new friends, and we all realized that we were not the only ones with problems.

One of the men at the first meeting was a guy who was in the process of divorce, bringing up two sons and a very young daughter. He was just beginning to deal with the realization that his ten-year marriage was over.

He had believed that he had a happy marriage, and was shattered when she left him with three young children, without any warning. Gradually, it seemed that we were often together, just talking, discussing problems, even sharing an occasional joke. After a few weeks, we decided to take my sons and his children to the local swimming pool. We spent most of the day together. The children seemed to get on, but we were both rather apprehensive.

There must have been some kind of mutual magnetism because, for the next few days, we seemed to spend as much time as possible together. We then went out for an evening on our own, no children to hide behind, just us. That was it – we knew we had to be together.

Friends told us we were mad, believing it was impossible to put seven children together, saying we should wait a while. My parents went berserk. They refused to acknowledge this man or his children. They were really concerned about my welfare, but they thought I should forget him and get on with my life as it was. I then had a decision to make. Them or him.

I loved my parents but, by then, I knew I loved him more.

In July, we went on a holiday together. By September, we were married. We bought a new house, and settled down, blissfully happy. Suddenly, our happiness was rocked by his ex-wife , who announced she was going to fight for custody of his three children. We couldn't believe it. There was no way we were going to let anything split the happiness of our family.

We found a solicitor and a barrister, and we were prepared to sell the house; we were going to keep those children. No one gave us a chance – everyone told us that the courts always favour the mother. It was a long, drawn-out battle, full of sleepless nights and tears; but, throughout it all, determination.

In the middle of the custody battle, we had a new arrival. Our daughter arrived in June 1983, completing our family. Also, my parents came to see us, realized how happy we all were, and we sorted out all our past troubles.

Over these months, the cloud of the custody battle

loomed. However, slowly, the powers-that-be realized the strong bonds of love we had, and after thirteen months of help, we walked out of court with our family intact.

We've been together now for six years. We now only have five of our brood left at home. The eldest is engaged, the next is the proud father of twins, and the third is away at college. They all come home for Christmas, which is terrific.

All we want to say is that no matter how hopeless the situation, there is always hope – there is always light at the end of the tunnel. We believed in each other, and we conquered all the odds.

Julie

'Julie also saw her love go sadly wrong. She found forgiveness. But she realizes the hardest part is rebuilding trust.'

[BROADCAST: MARCH 1989]

> *You are the sunshine of my life*
> *That's why I'll always be around*
> *You are the apple of my eye*
> 'YOU ARE THE SUNSHINE OF MY LIFE'
> –STEVIE WONDER

In May 1976, I came to London from Yorkshire to train at Great Ormond Street Children's Hospital. After three weeks at a nurses' home, my friend and I decided to share a flat. I used to travel to the hospital every day on the Tube. It was on one of those trips that I noticed a tall, good-looking clerk in the ticket office. He'd occasionally wave and smile, and I'd wave back.

One day, he called me over to chat, telling me that he'd also trained as a nurse, but had had to give it up because of poor pay. He invited me out for a coffee when I finished work, and the friendship grew from there.

He told me his name was Amal. One of the nicest things about him was his great sense of humour, and he just loved talking to people. Within a few months of knowing each other, I moved into his flat. We faced a lot of problems with our respective families – cultural differences, religion, different attitudes. He was Muslim, and most of his brothers and sisters had had arranged marriages. He was expected to follow suit.

Well, we eventually overcame some of the problems, and we married in the Autumn of 1978. I have three beautiful children, two boys and a little girl. In 1986, Amal decided to set up his own business – a shop in the East End. To help out financially, I said I would do some child minding.

Amal would got out to work at seven a.m. and come home at about nine p.m. We hardly saw each other. He'd come home every night complaining about the long hours and the hard work. One day, I got an anonymous phone call, saying that Amal had been seen in a fast-food shop with a woman. I confronted him with it, and he laughed! He told me he worked such long hours, he would have no time for an affair. I believed him, and trusted him completely.

Then, a few weeks later, I rang the shop. As he was talking, I heard a woman scream, 'Is that your wife? I want to speak to her!' Then the phone was cut off.

In an absolute state of shock, I bundled the children into a taxi. I was feeling numb. We arrived at the shop, and I confronted a young, very attractive girl of about twenty making a quick exit.

The next part of my story, a lot of people will find very hard to accept. We went back to her flat, leaving the children with their father. We talked for two hours, very civilized and calm. She told me she had not known he was married, and that she loved him very much. She flashed an engagement ring.

My husband took me home, and I asked him to leave. He packed a bag and went to his girlfriend's flat. I spent one of the loneliest nights of my life. I was devastated. I had a bath and put the children to bed, telling them how much I loved them, and how much their daddy loved them.

I cleaned the house, then sat down on the stairs with my cat, and a bottle of brandy. I felt lonely, betrayed, and I'll never forget the sight of my husband leaving with his suitcase. I felt *nothing*.

Thank God for friends and the Samaritans. In the early hours of the morning, I rang my friends and then the Samaritans. I don't recall any details of the conversation, but it was wonderful to speak to another human being.

I don't know how I survived the next few weeks. But I did. My husband came to visit every evening, and I could never look at him. I just felt it was the end of our marriage – ten years down the drain.

When he left, the children would run up to the door, crying, 'Why can't daddy come home?' It was awful.

During the next couple of weeks, he left his girlfriend and went to stay with his sister. He continued his daily visits. I didn't want the children to suffer. After all, they loved their daddy.

One morning, after dropping the boys off at school, my daughter announced she wanted to visit her daddy. So we drove down to the shop. The sight of that little girl running along the path really tugged at my heart-strings.

He came back to stay a few days later. He'd come to see the children as usual, but as he went to leave, I told the boys to run and ask him if he'd like to stay. Well, I have never seen my children move so fast.

A lot of people say that it's not wise to stay together for the sake of the children, but I think there was more to it than that. Life is certainly not perfect. How do you trust your partner again when he has been unfaithful?

But life goes on. Amal and I are back together again. I don't know what the future holds. Hopefully, time will heal. Although I love him, I can't forgive him.

However, I have just received a new wedding ring from him, inscribed: *Happy Tenth Anniversary*. I honestly believe now what I believed then, that he really is once again 'The Sunshine of my Life'.

Jane

'People will often try to turn a blind eye to the truth or tell little white lies in the hope of sparing heartache. That happened to Jane, in the worst possible way. But, in the end, everything turned out just right for her.'

[BROADCAST: JANUARY 1989]

> I want to reach out and know that
> you're there
> I want you to be the first thing that
> I see
> I want to wake up with you
>
> 'I WANT TO WAKE UP WITH YOU'
> –BORIS GARDINER

My story starts when I was just seventeen years old, and working as a waitress at a four-star hotel in the South Coast. While there, I met Brian. He was a waiter, and what a dish he was. Six foot, blond, blue-eyed and very kind.

We started seeing a lot of each other, and in 1982, we were married. It was bliss. We bought our own flat, and the only trouble started when we tried to have a family. I became pregnant the first time, but unfortunately miscarried. The hospital strikes were on at the time, and with no treatment, I was discharged. A year later, after trying with no luck, I went into hospital for an exploratory examination. They found both my tubes were completely blocked, and said I would have to have an operation to unblock them.

But, lo and behold, they must have moved something, because two months later, I found myself pregnant again. We were over the moon. It was not to be. At three months, I miscarried again.

We were shattered. Our marriage started to shake. Brian started to ignore his own appearance, and spend all our money gambling and drinking. Then, late one night, I decided that I had had enough. I tried to leave. I didn't want to go for good. I just wanted to shake him up a bit.

But he beat me black and blue, and said that he was glad I was going because his *boy friend* didn't like him being married. He was *gay*, and had been sleeping with other men as well as me. All my friends knew before we were married that he was gay, but they'd said nothing because they didn't want to hurt me. They thought I might know, but I never suspected anything.

I moved into the hotel up the road where I had been working, and got a live-in job. I was so lucky that the staff were all so kind to me, and really helped me through the most traumatic time of my life.

My divorce was final in five months, the grounds were so good! So there I was, twenty-three years old, and set to start a new life. But how could I? The two people I needed most in my life had been turned against me by my husband – who told them that I had been responsible for the break-up of the marriage.

After six months of hiding in my room, and trying to shut out the rest of the world, friends from the hotel finally persuaded me to venture out for a quiet drink in the pub on the other side of the road. It was great – a little strange at first, because I had forgotten what living was really like. From there we went to a nightclub where I met Tom, the barman from the pub. He had followed us.

We hit it off straightaway. We had so much in common: fishing, horse-riding, walking. I knew then he was someone special. I told him everything about myself, and he listened. For the first time in a long time, I felt wanted again. A few months later, we got engaged, and I tried to introduce him to my parents. My father was very rude. I gave them up as a bad job, and Tom and I moved to Wales, where we made plans to marry.

But we had a problem. His family were very strong Catholics and we were not allowed to get married in the church he wanted because of my divorce. But Tom stood by me, yet again telling me how much he loved me, and that things would work out. We rented a small house near his parents, and settled into our new life. I had a good job as a restaurant assistant about five miles away, and Tom got a job.

It was a month later that I became pregnant. We now have our son – which really put the icing on the cake of our happiness. We are due to be married soon in a register office.

My story is to thank Tom for standing by me, and for giving me what I never thought I could have – love, and a very special little boy. 'I Want to Wake up with You' just sums up exactly how I feel about Tom.

Melanie and Nigel

'When couples find love the second time around, there are often terrible pressures – especially when children are concerned. Melanie and Nigel found out just how terrible the pressures can be.'

[BROADCAST: JANUARY 1987]

> How can the light that burned so bright
> Suddenly burn so pale
> Bright Eyes
>
> 'BRIGHT EYES'–ART GARFUNKEL

Although my story has a very sad ending, I hope to God that one day it will reach a happy conclusion. I met Nigel in November 1979. I hadn't had many boyfriends, and I was in my first job. Nigel was getting a divorce, and was coming to the end of a long career in the Armed Services. There was quite an age gap between us, but to this day that has never worried us.

I liked Nigel instantly. He was from Liverpool, and a complete joker and charmer. We were so attracted to each other. But, underneath this kind wit and humour was a man in a great deal of emotional pain, which he still suffers from some eight years later.

He told me all about his divorce, how one day he returned home to find a letter from his wife on the kitchen table, saying that although she still loved him,

211

she felt their marriage wasn't right. She had left, taking their two daughters with her.

His eldest was aged just four, and the other ten months. He was devastated by it. After several months of not knowing where they were, he finally got into court to arrange access visits to the girls. By this time, Nigel was posted to Shropshire, and the girls were a long way away in Liverpool.

But we carried on seeing each other, and he introduced me to his daughters. When he bought a house in Shropshire, the girls would come and stay at weekends. They really loved their visits.

It is an understatement to say that Nigel's ex-wife became a thorn in our sides. I feel that we truly tried to allay her fears about Nigel having access to the children, but it was never enough. Access became a constant worry for Nigel.

But, with all the obstacles, our relationship flourished, and in December 1982, we got married. Nigel left the Forces, and in a bid to start a new life, he took up a new job which took us to New Guinea.

Although we were on the other side of the world, we constantly wrote to the girls, and they to us. Nigel missed them ever so much. But our dreams of a new life were shortlived, and we returned to England within only fifteen months. Nigel's joy at seeing the girls again was tremendous, but all too soon the stress of seeing them on a regular basis became apparent once more, and put a great deal of stress on our relationship.

These difficulties reached a climax in July 1985, when we had to go to court to fight for the right to take Nigel's children on holiday with us to Scotland. Thankfully, the judge supported us, saying that Nigel was a very good father, and there was no reason the girls couldn't go.

But, during that holiday, I did a lot of thinking. I felt

I could not take the problems anymore. I had begun to resent the children, because of the trouble just seeing them caused. At the end of the holiday, the eldest cried and pretended to be ill because she didn't want to go home. That was the last time we were to see Nigel's children again.

In September, just weeks after that holiday, Nigel was in court again. This time his wife wanted to change the times when we picked the children up at weekends. We usually picked them up on a Friday evening, but she wanted it changed to Saturday mornings, so effectively we would be losing most of Saturday travelling to and from Shropshire.

But Nigel was pushed into a corner, where he either accepted the new regulations or risked losing his rights to see the children. Nigel was weary and dejected after six years of battling for his rights to continue seeing his children, and couldn't carry on anymore.

Everyone, including myself, told him that it would be 'for the best' if he didn't see his kids anymore, and that he would 'soon get over it'. That was over three years ago, and he has not heard a word from them ever since.

It was not long after that he realized he had made a terrible mistake, but if you can understand how he had battled for six years with people telling him to stop seeing his children, then I think you'll see the insurmountable problems he faced.

Eight months after the court case, I became pregnant. In my heart of hearts I hoped our own children could halt his feelings of pain and despair over losing his two children. But even before the birth of our children, Nigel was taking steps to try to go back to court to see his girls. He wanted to redress the mistake about which he felt so guilty.

In the months following the loss of his children, I realized that Nigel behaved like half a man. It was as if a part of him had curled up and died. When we talked about it, I knew that his hope lay in the fact that he might be able to see the girls again one day.

In March 1987, our son was born, and Nigel was looking forward to the day that he could introduce him to his stepsisters. But that day never came.

In September, after two gruelling trips to Liverpool, a different judge ruled that it was in the best interests of the girls if they did not resume contact with their father ever again. Nigel was shattered. He wasn't allowed to see them, and the judge said he could only send Christmas and birthday cards. Nigel hasn't done anything wrong, so how could they do this to him? Even criminals in prison aren't stopped from seeing their children.

Perhaps this letter will reach the two young girls – now thirteen and a half and nine and a half – and tell them that their daddy still loves them very much, and, against all odds, he has tried to see them. Of course, we have our own child, but I hope that one day his two girls will seek him out and make his happiness complete.

In earlier days, 'Bright Eyes', by Art Garfunkel, was his eldest daughter's favourite song, and she once said to him, 'Daddy, whenever I hear this song, I will think of you.'

To this day, tears still fill his eyes when the record is played.

Jane and Alistair

'While people say that love consumes all, jealousy is the one emotion that seems to destroy everything. I have received so many letters about jealousy – real or imagined. Jane and Alistair's story shows how jealousy can sometimes build up.'

[BROADCAST: SEPTEMBER 1989]

> *I've wasted all my tears*
> *Wasted all those years*
> *And nothing had the chance to be good*
> 'HOLDING BACK THE YEARS'–SIMPLY RED

I know my problem is nothing compared to some of the stories I have heard on your show, Simon, but I want to tell it anyway. I had been married to Alistair for nearly six years, hopefully very happily. We had a beautiful baby boy in the summer of 1988.

We were both filled with joy when he was born, and no one could have been more proud than his father. But we both loved him dearly.

In that September, Alistair got a new job, and I was very proud of him. But, then, that pride turned to jealousy in such a way that I just couldn't stop. I suppose because he was meeting so many people, so many 'girls', and knowing Alistair is the friendly type, he obviously got on very well with everyone.

I just couldn't stand it. I questioned him to no end

about the most trivial of things. Being at home all day with an eighteen-month-old baby, I suppose there isn't much to do but think. The more I thought, the more convinced I was that he was doing the dirty on me.

Alistair always denied that he would do anything against me, but that wasn't enough. I still kept on. Then, Alistair stopped denying it. In fact, he just stopped talking, which made me even more jealous. Things got pretty bad for a few weeks, but still I carried on questioning him.

Then, one night, I told him just to go, all the time thinking he wouldn't dare. I was wrong. He did go. Luckily, he turned to his family, who obviously listened to him, and, being the kind people they are, listened to my side, too.

That's when I realized how much I had hurt Alistair with my accusations and temper. Alistair did come home the next day, and we talked. I thought I could stop being jealous overnight, but no, I still had to have a little go here and there.

Eventually, after about a week, we talked again. But, this time, Alistair said he had had enough, and that he didn't want to try. Hearing that hit me like a brick. I was literally heartbroken, believing he didn't love me anymore.

I couldn't imagine that I had had anything to do with his feelings. Now I know I must have hurt him deeply. He even started lying to me about silly things, knowing that I would build incidents into something they weren't. And, because I knew he was lying, I thought there must be 'another woman'.

All the time, I couldn't believe that I was causing this trouble. We are still together, and have said we are going to try. I know I have got to try to regain Alistair's trust, and I realize that I must be made to feel secure in the relationship.

I suppose my message to anybody who is very jealous of their partner is that not showing them how much you care and love them will just destroy the trust and feelings your partner will have for you.

All I can say to Alistair is how sorry I am for all the things I said to him, and that I love him more than anything. 'Holding Back the Years' will tell him how I feel.

Kathy

'Kathy found the greatest strengths in her husband in the face of the worst adversity.'

[BROADCAST: JUNE 1986]

> *Any any time you feel the pain*
> *Hey Jude, refrain*
> *Don't carry the world upon your*
> *   shoulders*
>
> 'HEY JUDE'–THE BEATLES

It was 23 August 1987. I was twenty-six weeks pregnant with our second child, already having a beautiful two-and-a-half-year-old son. We were driving our new family car, and we were involved in a head-on collision.

Luke, our eldest, sustained a broken leg and a serious head injury, which left him with a blood clot on the brain. He was rushed to the local general infirmary for emergency surgery on the brain, and taken to intensive care after the operation. My husband and parents were told to expect Luke to be brain damaged, and also in a coma. The longer the coma state, the worse the brain damage. By some miracle Luke came around the next day; although still very poorly, he recognized everybody who knew him, which was brilliant and more. He even had the spirit and courage to tell his distraught dad not to worry, which left dad in floods of tears.

Jeff sustained bad cuts across the chin, and cracked ribs, which he brushed off as just minimal. I suffered a fractured hip, and jaw cuts and bruises. I was thrown into premature labour, which the hospital was able to subside. I was losing a lot of blood, which was a great worry at the time. At this time, I didn't realize how seriously Luke was injured – or for the next two weeks – because I was heavily sedated for the baby's sake.

I was in traction and my jaw was wired. I hurt from the wallop I'd taken. I was bedridden for seven weeks, and then on 12 October 1987, at thirty-three weeks pregnant, I was taken for an emergency Caesarean section, and Matthew was born. But it doesn't end happily I'm afraid. He was born physically and mentally handicapped. Jeff, my husband, had the most dreadful job of explaining Matthew's problems to me, which must have been horrific for him. I was, to say the least, devastated. Jeff had to tell me that Matthew might not make it through the night because he needed seventy-five per cent oxygen. All of the seven weeks I held on to him, I hoped he would be all right at the end – but fate was against our struggle! I was discharged from hospital and Matthew came home three weeks later.

We tried to get our lives back to normal, pretending things hadn't really happened. Matthew was going to be normal, the doctors must have been wrong. We love him, he can't be handicapped, surely! But the truth has to be faced sometime, and as time wore on it was apparent he was mentally and physically handicapped – his problems becoming larger and larger to cope with. It ripped apart us and almost our marriage. Jeff coped well with things at first; he didn't have time to sit and think whilst visiting the hospital and caring for Luke and me when we came home – I was on a zimmer. Then, Matthew came home and that was three of us to care for.

Obviously, as time wears on, realization comes to the top and Jeff's guilt, although the accident was not his fault, sickened him. I wanted a knight in shining armour to come and take me from the nightmare, this lasted about nine months. Then, after a few sessions with a psychologist I realized that Jeff was that man. I started to realize that Jeff blamed himself for my injuries, Luke's injuries, and also Matthew's problems. I was being so selfish I didn't realize he needed loving and nurturing; I thought he was fine. But, Jeff, you are the bravest, most compassionate, loving and caring husband and dad I've ever had the fortune of meeting and loving.

Up to date: Matthew became too much to handle for me and has been, agonizingly, placed with foster parents. His future is yet undecided.

Luke has made a fantastic recovery, and has had a silicon plate placed over the hole left in his skull. He is not brain damaged. He's fantastic and normal.

Jeff and I are working hard on our marriage. We hit rough times – financial and emotional – but we are determined to make it work for Luke's and our sake. Please advise parents to use seatbelts, because Luke would not have been here but for the seatbelt.

Please play 'Hey Jude', by The Beatles – it is very special to him. Cut out of it what you feel should be unsaid, and use our names if you want to.

Nigel and Melanie

'Illnesses may sometimes seem overwhelming to some people, but they may not be quite the problems they seem. Nigel and Melanie, from Sussex, proved that point.'

[BROADCAST: MARCH 1989]

> No I won't be afraid
> No I won't be afraid
> Just as long as you stand by me
> 'STAND BY ME'–BEN E. KING

I need to tell you, Simon, that I think 'Our Tune' opens my eyes every day to the plights and problems of other people – and really helps people cope. That's why I hope my letter will help other people in a similar situation come to terms with the problem.

My story starts in 1987. It was shortly after my eighteenth birthday, and I was out on the town, celebrating with my brother and a friend. I'd had a few to drink, and so had the other two. Then my friend introduced me to a lady, called Melanie, who literally took my breath away.

When she stood up, I was so shocked, because she was very small and used crutches. When she went to the toilet, I asked her friend about Melanie's disability. He told me that she had spina bifida. Far from deterring

220

me, though, I thought more and more of her, because it was love at first sight on my part.

I started to go to the same pub every week, in the hope of seeing her again. But it took me almost three months to ask her out. You see, I'm not really that goodlooking, being a bit fat, and not having too much confidence. But she astounded me by saying yes.

One thing led to another, and that night we ended up kissing and cuddling. Believe it or not, that night, I met her parents, who took to me as quickly as I took to them. The only problem was that Melanie's disability was a very taboo subject with all the family, including Melanie, when she was with them.

The next day, I returned to her house after a driving lesson, and she told me that she would be leaving soon, to go on a holiday to Spain. Obviously, I said that that was great, but inside, I was really cut up.

I had really taken to her. As soon as she left with her mum, dad and sister, I began to miss her, even though we had only been together for less than a month. She phoned me every night. I counted the days to the moment she would come back, and, when she did, she assured me that she still felt the same about me as I felt about her.

She met my mum and dad, and they liked her a lot as well. But, they did take me to one side to warn me about all the responsibilities I was taking on if this was going to become serious.

We fell in love pretty quickly, and got engaged in that July. It was on Melanie's birthday. Even though we had only been going out for a few months, we both knew it was right.

Time passed. With my help, Melanie began to open up and talk about her spina bifida. She felt able to talk about her physical problems without becoming upset. Then, I started to run before I could walk. I began to talk to her about how much I would like to have children. Melanie became nervous and irritable.

She told me that she didn't want to have children, and that we weren't going to have any. I was pretty brassed off, as you can imagine, Simon, and things became really strained between us.

We quarrelled and made up, split up and reconciled. Then, one night, during a really heated argument, she broke down and told me that she really *did* want to have children. The reason she had said no was because she didn't know if she *could* have them or not.

It made me think what a selfish person I was. I'd never given those feelings of Melanié's a single thought. I did some serious soulsearching, and told her that I loved her so much, it was totally her decision whether or not she had children.

I said I'd stand by her all my life, whether she wanted to have children or not. At the moment, we have set a wedding date in five months' time. Melanie is now a lot more open about her disability, and we are both very, very happy.

We still have to find out whether or not she can have children, but it doesn't matter to me anymore, as long as I can have her. 'Our Tune' is the song that was playing in the pub when we first met: 'Stand by me'. It says it all for us.

I just hope that people realize disabled people have feelings, and are just as much people as you and I.

Afterword

What you have just read are only some of the many letters that I have kept safely over the years. And, every day, more and more letters pour in. People often write to ask what's happened to the writer of a particularly moving letter. Most of the time, I'm sorry to say, I don't know.

But, that isn't always the case. More often these days, people are taking the time to write to 'Our Tune', and to tell us all what has happened since they first wrote.

One particularly happy example is from Kathy and Jeff, who wrote to me from Buckinghamshire:

Dear Simon,
I don't know if you remember. I wrote to you in August 1984. Jeff and I were going through a really bad patch in our marriage. He was a travelling salesman, and was never at home – always on the road making his rounds.

I asked you to play 'Baby I'm a Want You', by Bread, telling you how I thought this was the last chance to save our marriage. I knew Jeff would be in his car that morning, and would be listening to your show.

That afternoon, I knew something was up when I heard his car pull up in the drive. He never came home before seven o'clock. The door opened, and I heard him call me out of the kitchen.

He had a huge bunch of roses in his hand, and looked as though he were going to cry. In fact, he said he had been crying, all the way back down the M1 from Staffordshire.

223

He had heard my letter, and literally had to stop the car, he felt so upset.

He realized how selfish he had been in our marriage, and promised that whatever else happened, he would change for the better. He did, Simon, and we have never been happier together. It is the greatest marriage anybody could want.

Karen and Richard also managed to save their relationship, thanks to an 'Our Tune' request.

Dear Simon,

I have just got to tell you what happened after you played a record for me and Richard. We had broken up because he was beating me two or three times a week. Sometimes, he would really bruise me badly.

He heard my letter to you while he was working at the garage in Aldershot, where he was a mechanic. Even though you changed the names, he knew who you were talking about. I could never tell him to his face, because I was so scared of him. But honestly, he has changed completely now.

It has only been three months, but he hasn't hit me once, and seems as though he is making the effort. Thank you so much for taking the time to read my letter. You told Richard how much I loved him much better than I ever could.

Over the years, I think I have received letters from about thirty people who said that 'Our Tune' has helped to save their marriages. Joanna and Brian are a couple who, the last time I heard, were still together. This time it was Brian who wrote:

Dear Simon,

I cannot tell you just how happy I am at this moment. When Joanna first decided to write to you, we were going through some terrible problems.

I had been made redundant from work at the car plant in Coventry, and Joanna had to take up two jobs to make up the money. I was left all day in charge of the kids, and was getting more and more depressed. Some days I just didn't know how I was going to carry on – and had seriously thought of just walking out and leaving the family behind.

You know what it's like when you have to sit at home all day, and the rooms seem to get smaller and smaller and smaller. I felt like the whole place was closing in on me. The kids were getting on my nerves, although it wasn't really their fault. But the more depressed I got, the lazier I got.

I couldn't get myself up in the mornings even to think of trying to get another job. All I could do was get to the pub to have a couple of pints before I picked up the kids. But I did listen to your show in the mornings, and I don't suppose you remember playing 'I Will Survive' for us.

Joanna had written asking you to play the song, and telling you the story of how she feared my depression would eventually wreck our marriage. It did so much for me to listen to the song being played – and to her letter begging me to do something about myself – that I found the energy and the inspiration actually to get out there and get looking for work.

I'm now an assistant manager in a local supermarket, and although I'm not earning a lot of money, and Joanna still has to go out to work, at least I have got some respect back.

And, more importantly than that, I think that we are going to make it as a couple as well.

You've read about a number of people's experiences with adoption. It seems to be one of the most common problems – both for the adopted child, and for the parents who had to give up a child. Sometimes, just by hearing the details on the radio, families have found one another again. And, sometimes, it's easier to express feelings through another person.

Caron got in touch with me two years after I first read her letter:

Dear Simon,

You may remember reading out my letter in 1986 – and playing my 'Our Tune' record, 'Evergreen', by Diana Ross. I told you how I had finally found my mother, and met for the first time since I was adopted when I was six months old.

I was so excited at the time, that I don't think I told you quite how I felt about meeting mum for the first time. So, I thought I'd write to let you know that everything is still going brilliantly – and we are getting closer as the months go on.

Those first meetings – and I had only seen her three times when I wrote to you – passed by in such a blur that I don't really remember any details about them anymore. I can only think of someone who was middle aged, with a lovely open face, and a laugh that just filled me with happiness.

Since then, I have seen my mum at least three times a month, and it is fantastic. We share so many things in common. There is such a strong bond between us, I cannot even begin to wonder why it took so long for us to get in touch in the first place.

Some of our happiest times are when we go shopping together on a Saturday morning. We travel up from our home in Stanmore in Middlesex, and we browse through the stores all day long. The amazing thing is, she knows instantly what suits me and what doesn't. Mums know best!

Anyway, I just wanted you to know that things are going great, and if you get any other letters from people seeking their real parents, please, please, please read them out – they give so much hope during those long months while you're still searching.

Occasionally, I get letters from people who don't want to request a record for 'Our Tune' – but just want to express how happy they have been to hear one of the letters. This was one I got from Boston in Lincolnshire. For obvious reasons, I have changed the names:

Dear Simon,

Please don't read this letter out, but I just had to write and
tell you what 'Our Tune' has meant to me and my family.

The other week, you read a letter from a family, whose
daughter had been involved in a dreadful car accident. She
had been in a coma for a long time, but eventually had come
out of it, and was on the road to an almost full recovery. I
can't begin to tell you what that letter meant to me. My son
Allan was also involved in a car carsh.

It was shortly after his seventeenth birthday. One of his
friends – a bit older than him – had decided to take a group
of them out for the night. He had one of those fancy
sportscars and, unfortunately, although he had not been
drinking, he crashed.

Poor Allan was trapped in the wreckage for more than an
hour. He had broken bones in his back, and had internal
injuries. But, the worst thing was that his head had been hit
by a piece of metal that had come through the windscreen.

For more than six weeks, I sat at his bedside day and
night, praying that he would regain consciousness. It was a
terrible time. My husband Roland was ever so supportive,
but there is so little we can do.

One morning, he begged me to go home to get some
proper rest. That is when I heard the 'Our Tune' from the
other family. I'm not sure, but I think their record was 'Let
it Be'. It touched me so much, I cried and cried in the car
on the way home. But, more than anything, it made me
determined never to give up talking, touching and kissing
Allan, in the hope he would respond.

After seven weeks, he did. Although he is not well yet –
there is a lot of work to get his muscles operating properly
– he is about halfway there.

I had to tell you how much encouragement and hope that
letter gave me, and how much hope it must have given other
people.

Letters like these make 'Our Tune' so worthwhile.
And that's the reason why I'll be sure to keep 'Our
Tune' for a good few years yet. As long as listeners

continue to write in, and to find something special in the programme, 'Our Tune' will be an important part of my show.

There is one special area that has grown over the last few years – letters from parents who have discovered that their children are gay. Jackie and Tom – I won't say where they came from – discovered the truth about their son, but asked me to play an 'Our Tune' to tell Jeff how much they still loved him:

Dear Simon,

When you read 'Our Tune', I think we were at the bottom of the barrel as far as our feelings were concerned. But, when you read out our letter, it just changed everything between us and our son, and hopefully will make everyone understand each other a little better.

It is very difficult when you come from a middle-class background, where nothing unusual ever happens, to discover that your only son is gay. The shock, as we told you, was so severe that Tom refused ever to speak to Jeff again.

But, you cannot stop loving somone just because their lifestyle isn't the same as yours. When you played 'You've Got a Friend', by James Taylor, for us, and read our letter saying that we would still always be there for Jeff, it was like a dark cloud lifting from over the family.

I had written a letter to Jeff, asking him to listen to your show on the day you said you would broadcast it. For two days, I didn't hear anything; then, out of the blue, the doorbell rang, and there he was.

He just smiled, held out his arms, and hugged me. I can't remember when he ever expressed any emotion like that to me. I couldn't help crying. We hugged each other for what seemed like ages, and then he sat down and talked to me – talked about his life, his feelings, and why he had kept everything bottled up for so long.

It was a Sunday afternoon, and when Tom came home, he also held Jeff. He finds it harder than I do to accept Jeff's lifestyle, Simon, but as the song told our son – we will always be there for him.

And that's what love is all about. Thank you so much for helping us.

The letters you write to 'Our Tune' can have the names changed, or left as they are. It's up to you. It's amazing how many people's lives can be affected by a few, heart-felt words, and by others' stories of survival. When people suffer great sadness or tragedy in their lives, and manage to pull through it, their stories offer extraordinary inspiration to listeners suffering similar problems. Likewise, stories of happiness and miracles can brighten the days of those who are finding them difficult to pass.

Continue to write and request your tune; sometimes just writing the letter will help to put things into perspective. I read every letter that comes through this door, and I try my best to play as many as I can.

'Our Tune' has just celebrated ten years of success. Let's make it another ten. I'd love to hear from you.

Simon Bates
July 1990

Acknowledgments

I'd like to say thanks to some wonderful people for making this book possible;

To Julie Hudson, who helped save me when times got tough;

To Claire, for all her help;

To Karen Hurrell who kept me going; and finally, a big thanks to Martin for bringing it all together.

Music Credits

Carry Me – Chris de Burgh –
  Composed by Chris de Burgh
Copyright © Rondor Music
(London) Ltd

Don't Turn Around – ASWAD
Composed by Albert Hammond
  and Diane Warren
Copyright © Albert Hammond
  Music and Realsongs

Diggin' Your Scene
  – The Blow Monkeys
Composed by Robert Howard
Copyright © Trash Songs Ltd

Hey Jude – The Beatles
Composed by John Lennon and
  Paul McCartney
Copyright © World by
  Northern Songs Ltd

Everything I Own – Boy George
Composed by David Gates
Copyright © Screen Gems –
  EMI Music Inc., USA

World Without You –
  Belinda Carlisle
Composed by Diane Warren
Copyright © Realsongs

Without You – Nilsson
Composed by Peter Ham and
  Tom Evans
Copyright © Apple Publishing
  Ltd

I Want to Know What Love is
  – Foreigner
Composed by Mick Jones
Copyright © Somerset Songs
  Publishing Inc and Evansongs
  Ltd

I Want to Wake up With You –
  Boris Gardiner
Composed by Ben Peters
Copyright © Ben Peters Music
  and The Welk Music Group
  Ltd

I Will Survive – Gloria Gaynor
Composed by Dino Fekaris and
  Freddie Perren
Copyright © Perren, Vibes
  Music Company

Nikita – Elton John
Composed by Elton John and
  Bernie Taupin
Copyright © Big Pig Music Ltd

No More the Fool
  – Elkie Brooks
Composed by Russell Ballard
Copyright © Russell Ballard
  Ltd/Virgin Music (Publishers)
  Ltd

*Nothing's Gonna Change my
  Love for You* –
  Glenn Medeiros
Composed by Michael
  Masser/Gerry Goffin

231

MUSIC CREDITS

Copyright © Almo Music Corp and Prince Street Music (ASCAP) and Screen Gems – EMI Music Inc

You'll Never Walk Alone – Gerry and The Pacemakers
Composed by Oscar Hammerstein II and Richard Rodgers
Copyright © T.B. Harms Co, USA and Chappell Music Ltd

Temptation – Wet Wet Wet
Composed by Graeme Clark, Tom Cunningham, Neil Mitchell and Marti Pellow
Copyright © Chrysalis Music Ltd/Precious Music

Three Times a Lady – The Commodores
Composed by Lionel Richie Jnr.
Copyright © Jobete Music Co. Inc. and Commodores Entertainment Publishing Corporation

The Power of Love – Jennifer Rush
Composed by C. de Rouge, G. Mende, J. Rush and S. Applegate
Copyright © Libraphone Musikverlag

Stand by Me – Ben E. King
Composed by Ben E. King, Jerry Leiber and Mike Stoller
Copyright © Trio Music Co Inc.

Never Gonna Give You Up – Rick Astley
Composed by Stock/Aitken/Waterman
Copyright © All Boys Music Ltd

Against all Odds (Take a Look at Me Now) – Phil Collins
Composed by Phil Collins
Copyright © Effect Sound Ltd/Golden Torch Music Corporation

A Groovy Kind of Love – Phil Collins
Composed by Toni Wine and Carole Bayer
Copyright © Screen-Gems-Columbia Music Inc.

World – The Bee Gees
Composed by B., R. and M. Gibb
Copyright © Abigail Music Ltd

Bright Eyes – Art Garfunkel
Composed by Batt
Copyright © April Music/Watership Productions

Sing – The Carpenters
Composed by Raposo
Copyright © Jonico Music

Love Action (I Believe in Love) – The Human League
Composed by Oakey and Burden
Copyright © Virgin Music

You are the Sunshine of my Life – Stevie Wonder
Composed by Stevie Wonder
Copyright © Jobete Music

Isn't She Lovely? – Stevie Wonder
Composed by Stevie Wonder
Copyright © Jobete Music

Walk on By – Dionne Warwick
Composed by Bacharach and David
Copyright © Blue Seas Music/Jac Music

MUSIC CREDITS

Head Over Heels –
Tears for Fears
Composed by Orzabel and
Smith
Copyright © Phonogram

You're my Best Friend – Queen
Composed by Deacon
Copyright © Trident Music

*Sorry Seems to be the Hardest
Word* –
Elton John
Composed by Elton John and
Bernie Taupin
Copyright © Big Pig Music Ltd

If You Leave Me Now –
Chicago
Composed by Peter Cetera
Copyright © BMG and Island
Music

Truly – Lionel Ritchie
Composed by Lionel Ritchie
Copyright © Brockman Music

*I Know You're out There
Somewhere* –
The Moody Blues
Composed by Hayward
Copyright © Bright Music

Big Time – Peter Gabriel
Composed by Peter Gabriel
Copyright © Cliofine

Don't Give Up –
Kate Bush and Peter Gabriel
Composed by Peter Gabriel
Copyright © Cliofine

*Donna, Waiting by the
Telephone* – 10CC
Composed by Godley and
Creme
Copyright © St Anne Music

The Glory of Love – Peter
Cetera

Composed by Cetera, Foster and
Nini
Copyright © Fall Line Orange
Music/Air Bear Music/Warner
Tamerlane Publishing
Corporation

Miss you Like Crazy –
Natalie Cole
Composed by Masser, Goffin
and Glass
Copyright © Screen Gems EMI
and Randor Music

Dinner with Gershwin –
Donna Summer
Composed by Russell
Copyright © Geffen and
Rutland Road Music

All out of Love – Air Supply
Composed by Russell and Davis
Copyright © Arista
Music/BRM/Riva

Hard to Say I'm Sorry – Chicago
Composed by Cetera and Foster
Copyright © Chappell and
BMG

Suddenly – Billy Ocean
Composed by Ocean and
Diamond
Copyright © Zomba Music

With or Without You – U2
Composed by U2 and Bono
Copyright © Blue Mountain
Music

Holding Back the Years –
Simply Red
Composed by Hucknal and
Moss
Copyright © CBS Music

Being with You –
Smokey Robinson
Composed by Smokey Robinson

MUSIC CREDITS

Copyright © Jobete Music
The Look of Love – Madonna
Composed by Madonna and
    Leonard
Copyright © Warner/Chappell

You to me are Everything –
    The Real Thing
Composed by Gold and Denne
Copyright © Screen Gems EMI

You've Lost that Loving Feeling
    – The Righteous Brothers
Composed by Spectre, Mann
    and Weil
Copyright © Screen Gems EMI

I Will Always Love You –
    Dolly Parton
Composed by Dolly Parton
Copyright © Owepar
    Publishing Co.

Something about You – Level 42
Composed by King, Badarou,
    Gould and Lindup
Copyright © Level 42 Music,
    Chappell Music, Island Music
    and Visual Arts

*You're the Best Thing that ever
    Happened* –
    Gladys Knight and The Pips
Composed by Weatherley
Copyright © Ardmore and
    Beechwood

Please Don't Go –
    K C and The Sunshine Band
Composed by Casey and Finch
Copyright © Intersong Music

Together We are Beautiful –
    Fern Kinney
Composed by Leray
Copyright © Bramton Music

For Crying out Loud – Meatloaf
Composed by Steinman
Copyright © Carlin Music

A Different Corner –
    George Michael
Composed by George Michael
Copyright © Morrisson Leahy

Here's To You – Billy Ocean
Composed by Ocean,
    Braithwaite, Eastmond and
    Skinner
Copyright © Zomba Music

River Deep, Mountain High –
    Ike and Tina Turner
Composed by Spectre,
    Greenwich and Barry
Copyright © Carlin

All Right Now – Free
    Composed by Fraser/Rodgers
Copyright © Blue Mountain
    Music

I Knew You Were Waiting –
    George Michael/Aretha
    Franklin
Composed by Climie/Morgan
Copyright © Chrysalis Music
MCPS/BLEM

St Elmo's Fire – John Parr
    Composed by Foster/Parr
Copyright © Copyright Control

Tender Hands – Chris de Burgh
    Composed by Chris de Burgh
Copyright © Rondor Music
    (London) Ltd

Your Song – Elton John
    Composed by John/Taupin
Copyright © Dick James Music